Do Not Try HIM at Home

SANDRA TEN HOOPE

First edition.

ISBN: 978-1-8381634-0-2

Ebook: 978-1-8381634-1-9

Published by the Quiet Rebel Bureau

Cover and Interior design by Lyn Thurman at the Quiet Rebel Bureau

www.quietrebelbureau.com.

DARE TO DISPLEASE PRESENTS

DO NOT TRY

HIM

AT HOME

Sandra ten Hoope

For Michiel and Jolanda,

Friendship beyond dimensions.

DO NOT TRY HIM AT HOME

ABOUT THE AUTHOR

Sandra ten Hoope is a storyteller, corporate lawyer, and toxic relationship recovery expert.

Her mission is to:

- Raise awareness that professional, high achieving, successful women, can end up in toxic relationships.
- Offer support to women who silently suffered in toxic relationships, managed to escape, and wish to rebuild their confidence and trust.
- Make women realise that they should never lead a should-driven life. Be you. Unapologetically.

You can reach Sandra at:

Facebook group:
https://www.facebook.com/groups/daretodisplease/

Facebook book page:
https://www.facebook.com/DoNotTryHIMatHome/

LinkedIn:
https://www.linkedin.com/in/sandratenhoope/

A note to you, the reader

HIM OR HE = HER OR SHE

This book is titled: Do not Try HIM at Home.

It describes my experiences as a heterosexual woman with heterosexual men who abused me in several ways: emotionally, physically, and financially.

Abuse, however, is gender neutral.

Men and women abuse. Men and women fall victim to abuse.

The 'him' or 'he' could also be read as a 'she' or 'her'.

Abuse is not restricted to male-female relationships.

It occurs in male-male, female-female, and all other kinds of relationships.

Abuse can hit you – literally – no matter where you were born, the colour of your skin, where you live or what you do for a living. Professional women and men also fall prey to abusers. Which adds an extra layer of shame – you, of all people, being abused?

View my story as a tale in which the 'I' could be anybody. It could be you; it could be someone you know. Whenever you get triggered by any of the stories, go to the resources chapter towards the end of the book. There, you will find an overview of help services in various countries around the globe.

CONTENTS

Introduction

Call me a storyteller, strategist, conscious catalyst, focus facilitator, awareness advocate, clarity counsellor, or transformation aide. My sole purpose is to provide women with the tools and solutions that allow them to be themselves again.

I am a certified Master at Law with over 25 years of experience. Some of the wealthiest people on the planet entrust me with their assets.

And yet, there was a time when I didn't entrust me… with relationships.

On the outside, I looked like I was in control. High achieving, professional woman. Behind closed doors? Well, that's a different story. It is my story. This I am glad that I'm able to share it with you and I hope that it helps you in some way.

Born and raised in Amsterdam, my childhood was shaped by a combination of factors, firstly being an unexpected arrival in my family alongside brothers aged 16 and 18. Predictably, this led to a major shift in family-dynamics, resulting in my parents splitting up when I was four.

Growing up, I was a shy, insecure, highly-sensitive, and intelligent child – otherwise known as an easy target at school. My escape was reading and learning and by the age of eight, I had already decided that I wanted to study law. So, when I finished school, I started to work as a secretary at a law firm whilst studying part-time.

After a few relationships, some more successful than others (including the one with the first HIM in this book), I landed myself a great, trustworthy, loving guy, yet I still could not settle. I was married at 26, then divorced at 30. Living abroad in the wonderful Caribbean Island of Curaçao, I discovered and relished a new part of myself – the passionate, energetic, dance-crazy part. One of my dance-partners, the second HIM in this book, tried to domesticate me. There are certainly spiritual advantages to a near-death experience caused by strangulation. My recommendation is, however, DO NOT TRY THIS AT HOME!

Once I had recovered mentally and physically (or so I thought) from this emotionally charged period of my life,

I fell in love again with a man who seemed attentive and caring – the third HIM you will encounter in this book. We were soon married and celebrated the arrival of my wonderful son. Yet, when my son was 18-months old, my husband left us. There I was – divorced again at 41.

I now had choices to make as it was no longer 'just me' – I had my son to consider. I could fester, I could wallow, or I could I pick myself up and remember who I was and that I was enough. I could finally dare to heal.

It took a lot of learning, primarily learning to love and appreciate myself for who I really was. I read voraciously and worked on my chakras. Then I realised that during my corporate career, as well as my 'real job', I had spent approximately 45,000 hours coaching team members or colleagues. I coached them on group dynamics, transformation processes, personal choices – life in general. Surely, I could use those skills to be a voice, to raise awareness on toxic relationships, to be a lighthouse for other women who had escaped?

This wasn't planned – it was just a natural development. A reflection of who I was, who I have become, the sum of every step of my journey. My mistakes, my successes, my learnings, my acceptance of my imperfections all placed me in a unique position where I could help others.

And now here I am! I took the plunge and started to write

this book, aptly named *Do not Try HIM at Home*. Writing this book has been a challenging yet also a healing journey. Through writing, I discovered my true purpose: to help fellow professional women who have survived toxic relationships. I want to help them rewrite their stories. To rewrite the scripts of their lives.

This book may make you laugh, cry, think, wonder, shiver – it is all good. You are not alone.

.

Him Number 1
THE WOMANISER

ROCK THE CASBAH

A regular Saturday night in November 1991. Out on the town with a friend. Food, drinks and hey, why not go for a little dance? We headed to a disco (yup, we called clubs 'discos' in those days) situated in a beautiful building on an Amsterdam canal. Lots of people, lots of laughter, lots of drinks. Who spotted who, I can't recall. But there he was. Handsome fellow. British. Northern accent. Would I like to dance? Sure. The first song we danced to was "Rock the Casbah," by the Clash. A prediction from above if ever I saw one... for he sold me a sweet story, like they do in a casbah. A place you are lured into. Many shiny objects. Slick talk. A hint of hidden treasures. Sultry whispers.

Your mind says, "Be aware, this is what the travel guide (aka your mom) has warned you about — if it looks too good to be true ..." But you want to believe. Kismet. Kiss whilst you have only just met. Another dance. It seemed like a fairy-tale. *1001 Arabian Nights*. We did not last that long though — the inevitable clash had already been written in the stars.

FALL AND RISE

My friend was staying with me that night. That blocked a potential after-party. We kissed and said our goodbyes. Would I like to have dinner the next evening? For sure. We met in a pizzeria. A rainy Sunday evening. We did not stay there for too long. He took me to the room he was renting (or so I thought), just around the corner. Reginald Perrin was on the telly. Oh universe, I know... that series was called *The Fall and Rise*. I rose to the occasion, feeling desired. I fell flat on my face soon though — lust is lovely, but not if you end up with an STD. And if only I had dared to admit to myself back then that it is okay just to lust after a person. That you need not convince yourself you are 'in love' to have a good time. That is how I was raised: girls only have sex with men they are in love with. A very dangerous belief inflicted upon me by not just my parents but also the media. All talked about love. Dangerous indeed. For with love comes all sorts of ideas and expectations. Commitments and obligations.

BELIEVE IN LOVE

Love. Sex. Love... it would not take long for him to come up with the story that the rent on his room was up and that he was now seeking a new place to stay. No guessing what happened next: I said, "But oh you can live with me." After all, we had already been seeing each other for 10 days or so. Remember, this was LOVE. A few days later he said that he was going to go out with his mates. Until that moment I did not mistrust people. He got home really late, five or six in the morning. I woke up as he entered thinking, "That is a bit late to come home from a night on the town." And then it hit me: a slight unrest. Distrust. Where had he been? Surely not with another girl? We had only been together for a few weeks; he would not cheat on me that quickly. My father had cheated on my mother after they had been married for 25 years. That, at least, was the story my mum had told me. I could sort of understand why they had broken up. Together out of necessity, not love. Two grown-up boys. Me as a big, unwanted, surprise. People would stray for less. But, if you are madly in love, only just met, a guy would not even think about other women. Surely not.

SURPRISE

Christmas came. He was going back to his folks in England. Yes, he would miss me deeply. As I would him. Which is why I got in touch with his mother and cooked up a little surprise. I would fly over just before New Year's. I made it safely to Manchester, took a taxi to the town where he lived. I couldn't wait to see the look on his face. The surprise was on me: he was not home. I did meet his mother, stepfather, and stepbrother. His mum told me a bit about his relationship history: a marriage, a daughter. She was adopted by his ex-wife's new partner while he was in Australia. From which HIM number one had been deported. I took it all in as if I were listening to a storyline from EastEnders. Wild men can be tamed, will be tamed, as soon as they truly fall in love. He entered the house around tea-time. Surprised to see me. Pleasantly? Not so much. It felt like I was in the way of his plans. Plans, as I found out a lot later, with names like Tracey, Marcy, Suzy... That night I asked him about his ex-wife. Yup, one day he came home, and she had left him. Took his daughter and everything in the house. Had not left a nail on the wall. I remember thinking, "Why would she have done that?" I came to understand why but only when it was too late.

New Year's Eve was fun. Cold. I remember waiting for the bus in the freezing fog. As I entered the bus, I saw that I was the only one wearing a coat. Everybody else was just in t-shirts. I met a few of his friends and I recall a few ladies casting strange looks as if to say: who the hell was I? I would ask myself that question often in the new year. It would turn out to be quite a year.

A STRAY DOG AND A MISSING CAT

Home we went, to Amsterdam. He kept going out on the town without me. The unrest grew and grew. I knew he had been with many women. I was stupid enough to play the 'how many did you have sex with?' game. When he said, "Over 100," I thought he was lying. It seemed impossible to a fairly new girl on the sex-block for a guy to have slept with so many. But it turned out to be an accurate number — he kept a record. A black book. I did not find out about it until later. Until too late!

I asked him, "After so many women, will just being with me be enough for you?"

"Oh, sure honey, I love you, really, I do ..."

Valentine's Day. He got me a cat. A cat! Oh yeah, I loved cats, but what a weird gift. The cat was lovely. He had collected her from an animal shelter. Her name was Josje and we bonded straight away. A few days later, he was meeting a few mates for drinks. I tried to fall asleep, but I couldn't. Ever since the first night when he'd come home late, I could not sleep until he entered the door. There were many long and lonely nights. Anxiety galore. This night, anxiety turned into sheer panic. I just had to know where he was. Had to find him. This is all in the pre-mobile era, so there was no way of telling where he was. I did know where one of his mates lived. I called for a taxi and went in search of him at a friend's house. It must have been 4am. He was not there. That friend was with his new girlfriend. She saw how stressed I was and managed to calm me down. We talked for hours. He'd told them that he really liked me. Perhaps he was just in one of those late-night bars?

I stayed with them until I could take the first tram home. He was not there. And where the hell was the cat? I could not find her anywhere. Panic struck again. She must have slipped out of the apartment in the night when I ran downstairs to catch the taxi. I searched all rooms, all cabinets, everywhere. Searched the streets. Called my mum, who was puzzled how the cat could have gotten away. My story of a night-time taxi-ride looking for him did not go down well with her. But the focus was on the cat. And as I said to my mum through my tears, "I really have no idea where Josje is," I heard a miaow from behind the curtains. There she was! I was so relieved. The stray dog, however, did not come home until late in the evening.

With a stupid story. That I chose to believe. Oh, the stories we tell ourselves. Way more harmful than any story anyone can ever throw at us. It would be okay. He loved me. I loved him. It would all be okay.

SHE CAN'T HELP IT, THE POOR THING

The phone rang. It was my friend wondering if I was okay. She had witnessed my total meltdown the night before. He had been late — again. In a state of panic, I had called my friend, who came over straight away. There I was screaming. Gathering his things together. No more of this. The insecurity. The lies. The feeling that I was going nuts. Which he made my friends believe as well. "She can't help but distrust me, the poor thing. Her father cheated on her mother, she learned to not have faith in guys from an early age." But everybody could see how fond he was of me, there's no way he would do me wrong. Oh, he played it right. Even my closest friends fell for his story and they worried for me. Not because of what he was doing to me, but for me not being able to trust him.

I felt so alone. And confused. Maybe I was wrong. Maybe he was not fooling around. Maybe it was all in my imagination. Those dreams in which I saw him drawing money from my account to go out with other women (he never had any money, kept losing his jobs). Those phone calls he would abruptly end. Maybe it was all in my muddled mind. Back to the breakdown. I had called my friend to come over. She found me, calmed me down and waited with me until he arrived home early, for a change. He comforted me, and her. When she called the next day, I just said, "Thank you, yeah, everything is fine now." But it wasn't. Not really.

FAMILY AFFAIRS

His stepbrother and nan came to visit us. She was a darling. Ran an unofficial gay bar in his hometown. I thought it would be fun to show them around some gay bars and to end the evening in a venue where my father played the accordion. Saturday night. There we were: the nan, the bro, and me. He was not home though. No message. Nothing. I said, "Right, then we shall simply go without him. Maybe he will catch up with us." The gay bars were fun — always a good vibe. Nan was in her element, Bro less so. We took a taxi to the final stop of that evening. My dad was pleased to see us. Even though neither he nor his girlfriend spoke any English, they got along with my temporary in-laws. We laughed, drank, danced... yet, I could not fully enjoy myself. I was worried. Where the hell could he be? He had stood me up a zillion times, but this was his family he was letting down.

Then the door opened.

There he was.

With... another woman!

Yes. Right there. In that bar. With all of us present. He had run in to a friend, he no doubt had told me about her, well uh.... They acted like very close friends. A tad too close for my comfort. I felt like I had landed in the wrong film. His nan looked like she wanted to kill him. As did my dad. Eventually we managed to get him into a taxi with us. He did not seem a bit bothered about the situation. And I? I turned a blind eye. Again.

BRIGHTON CALLING

Even before I had met him, I had booked a trip to England. I had always dreamt about sitting on the cliffs of Dover. There are weirder fantasies, for sure! So, off I went. For a week. Bus. Hovercraft. Youth hostels. I was really looking forward to this trip. I had never backpacked and would soon realise why. The low budget thing is truly not for me. But the towns I visited were good fun: Dover, Canterbury, Southampton, Winchester and finally, Brighton.

I had kept in touch with him on and off over the phone. In Brighton, I searched for a phone booth. He did not answer.

Decided to call my mum. She answered and she nearly bit my head off. "Come home," she said, "There is weird stuff going on with that guy of yours."

She had been to the house and there he was, with a bunch of English lads (he had stumbled upon them at immigration and had offered to rent them a room in the attic) and loads of women. Drunk. She had sent all the ladies packing and had told him in no uncertain terms that she would inform me. I panicked. Phoned him. Again and again and again. Still no answer. I ran back to the youth hostel, packed my stuff and headed to Gatwick Airport. Booked myself on the first flight to Amsterdam. He was home all right. Acting like a king in his castle. My mum was this and that and all sorts. These ladies had nothing to do with him, they were girls the English lads had brought home. But as my mum did not speak any English, she must have misunderstood. I chose to believe him. Again. Love is truly blind.

FROM PARIS TO HELL

I ran. Ran from my home. This was quite an achievement as I had just done a 24-hour bus trip to Paris and back. It had been a glorious trip. Just me, myself and joie de vivre. It had been a hectic few months. Living with him was exhausting. My trip to England was cut short because of his strange behaviour. I needed this day, badly. I was the only solo-traveller in a bus filled with shopaholics. I took the seat next to the driver, who chitchatted or rather shitchatted *all* the way to Paris. When I got there, I headed straight for my favourite church, La Madeleine. Reminiscent of a Greek temple, it only has small windows at the top of the walls. Shining a light from above — how appropriate. At the corner of La Madeleine, at the Fauchon delicacies store, I indulged in their signature tuna sandwich. I wandered the streets, drank tea and chocolate milk (coffee was not on my menu back then) and most of all, loved not having to involve myself in any conversation. Paris allows for anonymity — nobody wonders why you are there or where you are going.

The bus left again at midnight. I had informed him that I would be home at around 7am. The bus stopped at Central Station and I walked home. Made my way up the flight of stairs, opened the door, stepped into the bedroom and there he was. He and a she. Naked. Asleep. Well not for long. My primal scream most probably woke up the entire block. I yelled for her to get out of my house and whilst I could hardly contain my anger, I told him to get his stuff together and leave too. For whatever happened in the Bos and Lommer (our "hood") was not going to stay at the Bos and Lommer. Did not wait for them to get dressed and make their way out. I ran. Down the stairs. All the way to a friend's house.

I returned that evening. To an empty house. REST. I changed the sheets. Looked at a bottle of gin that I'd bought as a gift for a friend. Should I? But I realised that it would not stop the pain — it would only result in double trouble. Later that night, the English lads came home from work. They were awesome fellows, fully on my side. They had been wondering for months if I could see what he was up to. Or why I would accept it. We agreed: good riddance.

THE DIFFERENCE BETWEEN A DISCOMFORT AND A DISASTER

The story did not end there though. No, we did not live together anymore but I would still see him, either in my apartment or in the flat that he was renting. That is where I was on October 4, 1992. We had dinner and were watching the BBC news — I had been doing that since 1986 or so, I did not make a network-switch just for him. Then the presenter said, "Newsflash! A plane has just crashed near Amsterdam."

I almost went into shock. I had family who lived close to Schiphol airport. As it turned out, the area hit was in another part of town, the Bijlmer. The first footage hit the screens. An unimaginable disaster. Enough to make anybody forget about themselves and show compassion with the victims. Anybody, but him. He just couldn't stop ranting about how it was my fault that my GP wouldn't see him anymore. I had bad mouthed him to the GP. If a GP would choose sides, ever, it would have been mine. He's been my GP since I was four and still is. But my GP couldn't see him anymore because I had de-registered him from my home address. New district, new GP. A non-issue at the best of times. A disgrace that evening. When I was in a state of shock from seeing people dying on TV — he was worried about the one person that mattered to him: himself.

IT IS FOR YOU

The phone rang. A landline. Those were the days.

"Hi, my name is Miranda; can I talk to you about him?"

"Eh sure. He does not live here anymore though."

"I know," she said, "but I cannot find him anywhere and he has landed me in a right mess at work."

"Oh, what do you do?"

"I am an account manager at the ABN AMRO Bank and have twisted my manager's arm to give him a loan. But he is defaulting on his payments and they are blaming me."

"Oops, yeah, that is bad. He owes me money too, but at

least that is a private affair."

The doorbell rang. "Hold on Miranda, it's him."

He had stopped by to pick up some stuff. I opened the door downstairs and whilst he was making his way up and stepping into the living room, I continued my conversation with Miranda in Dutch. He always had plenty of Dutch courage but even after having lived in our dear country for a few years, he did not speak a word of Dutch. Miranda and I bonded, as you do. We even laughed. She had been in my house often she said. At first, she did not realise that he was living with a girlfriend. He kindly hid away my pictures when he was visited by Martha and the like. So many times, I had walked around my house thinking, "Hey, this is odd, this is not in its place." With my CSI mindset, I notice even the smallest change. I had even found earrings at the bedside table. "Oh darling, I did not have the time to wrap these for you, and I just bought them." Papers with phone numbers — yes, we are talking pre-mobile era. Nope, all work related. What work? The jobs he kept losing due to excuses like his nan having died. The smell of perfumes, not mine. Oh, mirror, mirror on the wall, how many women have passed my hall? Back to Miranda. I managed to calm her down a bit and then, after 25 minutes or so, I handed him the phone.

"It is for you ..."

BROMANCE

My friend, the one who had come over when I was losing my shit, was also going through a break-up. Both she and her HIM had been classmates of mine. I was there when they passed the 'friends to lovers' barrier. We were in our regular night spot. I had gone to the bathroom and when I re-entered the dance hall, I saw them together standing there. Holding hands. She had not even once hinted that she liked him. I walked up to them and literally tore them apart. Years later, she would tell me, "Your initial reaction was spot-on." After high school, they moved in together. She had stopped going to university and was working, whilst he was doing what he did best: not that much. Luckily, at some point, she woke up and threw him out. When she did, he started to sort of stalk me. Not in a romantic way: he considered me his line of communication with her. A stalk-stand in — I was moving up in the world of idiots. Fine by me, if he were on the phone with me, he could not call her. I stopped him from appearing in a new Dutch TV show where you could chase your ex with cheap flowers and fake excuses. I couldn't, however, stop him from going to a viaduct near her house and painting 'I love you, take me back' (including her name). All over the viaduct in great big letters! When he told me, proud as a toddler who had done his first poo on the toilet, I called her brother. He walked her home so as not to give her a heart-attack.

One evening, the stalker came to my house for a cup of coffee. My HIM stopped by as well. They hit it off like a house on fire. It only took them ten seconds to suck up to each other big time. They were such great guys. Smart. Handsome. God's gift to women. Hotter than Wham. Man, she and I were plain stupid to have let these two fine gentlemen go. If ever there was an 'Uh guys, I am sitting right here' moment it was that evening. Bromance! Homies at first sight. Narcissists do have it in them to praise another human being — provided that other person is a narcissist too. I was baffled. Was this really happening? Or was this *Candid Camera*? They went on for an hour or two. Then they left — off to a pub. Rumour had it that they even ended up on the same football team. HIM number one had been a keen player, at least by his own standards. After we had just met, he'd made me come to his club on Sunday mornings a few times. I still recall how cold I felt, standing there while he believed he was Gary Lineker. Far from it. When he asked me, "What do you think are the six biggest mistakes we made today?" and I gave a detailed account of at least 25 situations gone wrong, I was let off the football hook. If only I had unhooked myself completely.

ALL-NIGHT, CERTAINLY NOT ALL-RIGHT

The phone rang. Again. A sort of *Russian Doll* prequel.

"Hi, my name is Natasha, can I talk to you about him? I am his girlfriend and I feel like he is cheating on me. He did not come home again last night. I found his little black book (yes, he really had one!) and your name is on the top of the first page."

"Good morning Natasha, girlfriend is an ill-defined term when it comes to him. But if you are wondering if he is sleeping around, I can tell you: yes. I still do him occasionally and he spent the night here on Thursday. I have no idea though where he is now."

She started to cry and said, "Would you kindly come over to talk to me? I feel like I am losing my mind."

"Sure, where to do you live?"

She gave me the address, a narrow street in the De Pijp neighbourhood.

I jumped on the tram and walked into the quiet street — one of those lazy Sunday mornings. Just before I could press the doorbell, he walks towards the door too from the other side of the street. Lord knows where he had spent the night. When he saw me, he became really angry.

"What are you doing here?"

"Natasha invited me over for tea."

"But you can't go in."

"Oh, I can. For I have an inkling that Natasha's name is on the lease and that she is paying the rent — and for everything else."

In we went. Talk, talk, talk for hours. It was a mirror of the many drama scenes he and I had been through. She accused him of sleeping around. He denied it, fancy that. I could attest to it, but he still tried to convince her that I was lying. She cried. For hours. He kept on telling lies. A zillion lies. All of which I had heard repeatedly. It was reassuring and terrifying at the same time. It had not just happened to me. But it would certainly happen again to a lot more women after me. After her. There it was. The lightbulb moment: he would never change. He had lost his charm. For me at least. I left. No more booty or any other calls.

SO SORRY

In 2017, one of the guys who had lived in my attic sent me a Facebook message, "Hey, why won't you accept my friend request?" Oops, I hadn't recognised him. Anyway,

I was glad to see that he was okay. Now Facebook has this lovely tendency to bring your friends' friends to your attention. And vice versa. So, not long after the attic-lad and I had reconnected, a message popped up on Messenger. From HIM. Huh? It roughly read as follows:

"Hi. So glad you're healthy, happy and still red. I've been to Amsterdam en route to far flung places. I even went to the street where we lived to reflect. Basically, you were a lovely girl and I'm ashamed I didn't treat you as you deserved. I never forgot you, so am happy I can send this message. Your little boy looks lovely and you must be very proud. Bet you make a great mother. I still play football occasionally. Anyway. How are the white socks? Enough for now and very glad you're still on the planet."

"White socks?" I can hear you thinking. "What white socks?" Well, to date, I wear these when I go to sleep or else my feet get cold. This also applies to summer nights — only in a third week of a heatwave, I may not wear them for a night or so. A silly detail, yet obviously memorable!

I replied that I was indeed doing well. Thanked him for the apologies (friends said: is he in AA? Is this part of the recovery?).

He had once said that God had forgiven him. To which I had responded, "He is not the one to ask ..." I explained that yeah, he had treated me badly but that he had not won the Bad Guys in my life competition. Who had? Enter: HIM number two.

Him Number 2
THE ABUSER

THE FIRST DANCE

We met at a Sunday salsa party. Very popular evenings, attracting a big crowd. I was living in Curaçao (my company had sent me there for six months and as I had lived there before, I had said YES instantly) and was back in the Netherlands to spend time with my friends and family. A friend of mine went with me to the salsa. We had a couple of drinks and a couple of dances with several guys. Then he appeared. Asked me if I wanted to dance. Sure, that is what I was there for. We clicked dance-wise. No matter how experienced you and/or your partner may be, if there is no click, it will not work. We chatted a bit. And danced some more. I did not think that much of it back then. He also danced with my friend. When the salsa night ended, he offered to drive us to the bus-stop. Yeah, why not? He almost drove off without me — which still to this day scares my friend. But, when she yelled, "STOP!" he noticed that I had not yet sat down in the car. In hindsight, he may have been way more interested in my friend. Fully understandable, she was and is a gorgeous lady. He dropped us off at the bus-stop. We said our goodbyes. No numbers were exchanged. I went back to Curaçao a few days later, where I partied the night away with my then part-time lover. Did not think about him at all.

SUNDAY NIGHT FEVER

I returned from Curaçao earlier than planned, as my father was diagnosed with lung cancer. He did undergo treatment, but we knew he would not recover. As my new-build apartment was not ready yet, I moved in with a friend. As I was unpacking my things on a Sunday night, an urge to go out swept me off my feet. There was no rhyme nor reason — I was quite tired. But when the Sunday Salsa Fever hits you, you go. When I entered the club, I instantly saw him.

"Hey, what are you doing here? And where is your friend?"

"Working." Oh well, he seemed pleased to see me.

After a few dances and drinks, he suggested we go back to his place for a few more drinks. We kissed. Nothing more. This time, we did exchange numbers. I went back to my friend's place. The next day, I remembered that I had tickets for a Juanes concert. I called him, would he... yeah of course.

STAND IN LINE

The universe does send messages. And messengers. Angels. Sometimes disguised as gorgeous men — the kind you meet when on a date with someone else.

It was our first date: the Juanes concert. I had bought tickets without a certain 'plus' in mind. We had kissed and it was obvious we intended to hit a home run after the concert. I offered to get some drinks, ignoring that he had not offered to buy me any, and whilst the thirsty crowd shuffled to the bar, a guy started to talk to me. Handsome. Great energy. It turned out that like him, he also was Peruvian. In a few minutes we had spoken more than me and him had. And this guy said, "Did you ever feel like you have gone to an event with the wrong person?" Oh yes! But it felt so wrong to stand him up. To date, I think about this angel. If only ...

The Juanes concert was great, but him? Shit. Accusing me of improper dancing. He had smelled my weakness (shame and guilt) which triggered his inner hunter. I should have left him there and then. But I did not. Alas, we went back to his place. Or what I thought was his place. It turned out to be the house of one of his mates. He was doing some DIY on his house and he spent his nights here and there (which translates as: with one woman or another). In the car, the name-calling started. The way I danced. I had told him some stories about my life.

My marriage. After the first him, I had met a great guy — too great. There was no tension. No drama. I could not cope with a 'normal' relationship.

My divorce.

My then lover.

The lovers after that.

He threw everything at me – "How could you have betrayed your husband? All Dutch women are indecent." Oh, I should had walked away right then and there. But a part of me thought that he was right. I felt guilty about my marriage falling apart. Of not having fixed it, the mere brother-sister co-existence that it had become, before I had fallen for another guy. I felt guilty beyond belief. Guys like him prey on insecurities. They know exactly which buttons to push. Some end up on Wall Street. Other wolves play the game on another level. With him and me, the game was on. Big time.

We spent the night together. I left the next morning with a strange mix of excitement and disgust. Then, I set off on a huge quest for attention. Kept calling and texting him — old school mobile phones, no WhatsApp lights to indicate if the message had been read. He would never answer directly. If he responded at all, it was hours later. Always had an excuse — he was on his bike, working, whatever. I recall meeting him in a bar and he truthfully explained that he could not see us together. He had strong family values (notwithstanding that he was divorced) and I, like all white women, obviously only cared about loose relationships. This was true. I had come to understand that lust is not love. BUT, as he told me that I was nothing more than a slut, the 'I will prove you wrong' urge kicked in. I was going to make him see that I was a good woman. In general, and for him.

A BLUR

Months went by in which we saw each other occasionally. He was hardly ever kind to me. I do not remember too many details of that part of the story. As if the 'relatively normal' of that time has been overshadowed by the trauma that would follow. This 'normal' would see me doing whatever I could to get his attention. Good or bad. I got more and more accustomed to the never-ending name calling. Kept chasing him. I was basically asking him, begging him, to be kind to me.

At some point he called it off completely. He was going to Peru for a while and did not want to feel tied down to anything or anybody. I was busy with my new apartment. It turned out beautifully. He had indicated that he was going to be back around Queen's Day. When I heard about a salsa-party on that day, I sent him a text: was he going to be there? No response. However, I did see him at the party. He seemed happy to see me. He had received my text just after landing. What a coincidence! Dance. Drink. Sex. He had missed me so much. NOW we would make a real go of it.

MINDFUCK

He moved in. His house was still not finished. He had bought it, stripped it bare (and I mean BARE) and never had the money to properly do it up. But you guessed it, I loved helping him out. I started to pay his mortgage (as he always lost his jobs, never his fault, obviously), his child support, his everything really. Slowly but surely, he made me destroy all memories of the past. Pictures. Like my wedding pictures or any photographs of my ex-husband and the first HIM. He made me throw away a beautiful professional picture of children playing domino by a Curaçao artist. Even that made him think about the dark-skinned men that I had been involved with. Not a day went by that he did not mention my previous relationships. How could I have? I was nothing more than a white slut. Accused me of fancying almost every guy on the telly. Pointed out men on the street that I for sure had slept with — random strangers. To the point that I did not dare to look up anymore when we were walking or driving somewhere. Just kept staring at the ground.

Bashed my friends. All these Dutch women were as loose as I was. I should not see them anymore. Neither did they fancy spending time with him; he was far from sociable, to them that is. When it came to going out by himself, with his friends, he was ever so sociable. I started to see similar signs as when I was with the first him. I sensed so strongly that he was sleeping around. But of course, that was my dirty mind talking. I had not been trustworthy. I had slept around. I had not been a good girl. Not a decent wife. How dare I accuse him? I started to question my thoughts. Maybe I was wrong?

Obviously, this was a slow process. It is not like he moved

in and boom, I changed overnight. It is a devious mind-game. Mindfuck! He tapped into my insecurities, my shame, my guilt. Day by day. Adding pressure gradually. If you have ever seen documentaries or films about religious sects, this is a similar process. Also, when you watch an illusionist or hustler at work: they play with your perception. They twist what you believe to be true. They cash in on your blind spots. Mindfuck. Big time. Guys that abuse women use the same techniques. I slowly came to understand all of this many years later but not while I was living with him.

First, they charm you with their charisma. They seek out the parts of you that you wish to dislike. The shame. The hurt. The guilt. Little by little, they attack your personality. Emphasise that yes, you should be ashamed. Should feel guilty. Should be punished. Mould you into someone new. Someone that they can control. Someone who has no sense anymore about who they once were. Someone who has no clue how to escape from this hell. They isolate you from family and friends. People that could shed a light on the true you. You feel yourself slipping... but you are losing your grip. On the situation. On yourself. Shame kicks in about the situation as well. How could you, a successful woman, allow this kind of shit? You do not dare to tell anybody for fear of their reaction. Your world becomes very small. You are trapped.

PLAYING HOUSE

The day came that he brought his daughters to my house for the first time. They would stay with him every other weekend. Or rather, with his sister as his house was by no means finished. I would not see him during those weekends. Then one day, after a fight with his sister, he said, "Can they stay with me in your house? But I do not want you to be here straight away, let them ease into the situation." I stayed the night at my mum's. Late afternoon, he allowed me to come home. I still see their faces. The eldest in her early teens. The youngest was six. Lovely little ladies.

We got along fine and from that day on, they would spend every other weekend with us. We did fun things with them. However, they were also witness to the tension between me and him. He would also call me names in front of them. Alas, nothing new for the eldest as she remembered the relationship between her parents being challenging as well. I recall one day telling her, "I'm sorry, I'm not a good role model for you. When you grow up, make a boy respect you more than your father does me." Lots of years later, she told me that this advice had helped her considerably in her relationship choices.

As I became fonder of the girls, my tolerance for his emotional and mental abuse grew. For if we were to break up, I would never see the girls again. He sensed it. He made sure that he included the "either _____ or you will lose the girls" into almost every conversation. Conversations that were mostly fights. Or in all honesty, ALL conversations were fights.

NEW YORK, NEW YORK

As things seemingly went well between us (which translated as: I just kept quiet about all the shit things that were going on), he asked if I would like to visit the USA with him. A few of his siblings lived in New Jersey and he was going to take the girls there for a few weeks during the summer holidays. I could not join them for the full three weeks. They flew out there first. He had given me access to his Hotmail account so I could write job applications on his behalf. I wrote so many. He kept losing jobs. It was never his fault, obviously. Him not working was a huge financial burden. Then, whilst he was away, he received an email. From another woman. A poem. How much she missed him. I thought, "Huh?" Tried to call him about it. Could not get hold of him. When night-time came, he had changed the password to his Hotmail account. I had, however, copied the email.

Once I did speak to him, I asked: "Who is she?"

"Oh, an ex-girlfriend, insignificant."

I had my doubts. Doubted if I should even go to the USA. But the girls missed me so much. So, I did make the trip. I loved seeing the New York skyline as the plane landed at Newark airport. He was not there to meet me. Three hours later he showed up. He had been a bit busy that day.

His family was lovely. Hard working, kind people. His mother was a gem. His sisters treated me like part of the family from day one. They noticed how badly he treated me. They had seen this before when he was with his ex-wife. I could tell they felt for me. Although we might have been on holiday, we were not on a break from the usual name calling and other emotional attacks. He would go out at night without me. Just leave me there — entertaining the girls. I craved going into New York. He kept saying, "Tomorrow." Then one morning, after another fight, I walked to the bus stop and hopped on the first bus to New York. The moment I came out of the bus station on 42nd street, I felt at home. We basically see New York on television every single day. Either in the news or in a show.

The city vibe blew me away. As an avid *Sex and the City* watcher, I did what every fan of that show would do: went straight to the Manolo Blahnik store. I did not even need a street map (no Google maps back in those days!) to make my way round the city. The store felt like a candy shop. I did not buy anything though — I had never worn high heels. It was a wonderful day. I visited many stores. Went up and down the stairs in the Trump Tower. Walked around the park. It made me feel like ME again. I felt free. Vibrant. Alive even. I did not want to go back but I had to. He was very angry. I had upset his family who had been worried about me. How could I have just run away. I was so very irresponsible.

The sun had shone brightly in the city. Now, I was back in the shadows.

THE OTHER WOMAN

I flew home. A week later, he was supposed to land at midday with the girls. I thought he would be home at around 2pm but he did not get home until 7pm. I had tried to ring him. He did not answer. As I came in, I noticed that he had showered. I said, Huh?" Well, he had first brought the girls to their mums. And then he had gone to see his sister who was so curious how the trip had been. He had showered there.

We went back into our regular routine. I worked. Cleaned. Worried. One morning, it was 7am, he still not had come back from a salsa party. My CSI mind went into overdrive.

I searched for the "I miss you" email. Looked up the sender's name in the phonebook. It was quite a common surname but at the first name on the list I knew: this is her. She lived relatively close by, I decided to go there. At 8am or so. Dingdong. A woman answered.

"Hi, I am Sandra and I think my boyfriend is with you."

"Yes, he is. Do you want to come up?" she asked.

She lived on the third floor. As I entered the apartment, he looked at me.

"What are you doing here?" he said.

"Well, I think I should be the one asking that question."

She was the one who explained it all to me. They had been seeing each other for a long time. Even longer than he and I had been together. She had known about me. As he had described it to her: he loved her, but I could provide for him. I had a larger house, so his girls could stay with him. As it turned out, in the weekends when he should have been with the girls, he had first always dropped them at his sister's house whilst he stayed with this lady. Later, when the girls were with me, he had not been out with friends. He had been with her. Usually, he would sneak out in the middle of the night. But now, he had overslept. He had come to see her as soon as he had landed at Schiphol Airport. It was in her house, that he had showered.

She was a nice woman. Intelligent. Beautiful. I was not angry at her whatsoever. He had made me believe that he had been committed to me — nothing to do with her. Do not ever fall in the trap of blaming 'the other woman'! I did blame him though. Was ready to throw him out. Went to a friend to cry. She asked if I wanted to stay with her that evening, but I wanted to be in my own house. BIG mistake. For, of course, he showed up there. Drunk. Or so I now know, stoned. Totally devastated. He did love me. Just me. He was going to forget about this other woman. He and I were destined to be together. I did not give in, not instantly. I even went for drinks with that other woman. He was not staying with me nor with her. Neither of us knew where he was. We went to a salsa party together in the Vondelpark, dancing in the open air. As we were having fun, we suddenly saw him. In the middle of the dancefloor. With yet another woman. I lost it, then and there. Cheating on the both of us. What the hell? I walked up to him and confronted him. Which came as a right shock to the Latin salsa community where cheating was an unwritten rule. None of the men on the dancefloor were there with their wives or regular girlfriends. They looked at me as if I was an alien. I was so bloody angry! Up to that day, I had not known that I had a great number of Spanish swear words in my vocabulary. The third woman was in shock. All he could do was laugh.

BAD GRIEF

Meanwhile, my father was dying. The treatments had not worked. I was in despair. And, that was his way in again. He wooed me into taking him back. I was not fully concentrating on our story. I was too preoccupied with the imminent loss of my father. He was not at all supportive. I could not even discuss my hurt and fear with him. My father was taken to hospital. Even though they had been divorced for 30 years, my mum supported my father all through his illness. She called me in the early morning of Saturday, September 11, 2004. She was in the hospital with my father. The end was near. I took a taxi to the hospital. He never even offered to take me there. My mum and I stayed with my dad in his final hours. My brothers were not there — just me and my mum. After the divorce, they did not see much of my father anymore. We differ a lot in age. They were building their own families. My father was living his life. They knew about his illness, of course. But they were not there that day.

My mum and I laughed, cried, and told each other stories. Just after I had gotten to the hospital, my father, unaware of my presence, told the nurse, "Tell Sandra that I have always been proud of her." Those were touching words. And they would have made for memorable final words. But alas, his final word was coffee. He lost consciousness and was in a sort of twilight zone for hours and hours. At around 3:45pm, the daughter-in-law of his last girlfriend (she had died a few years earlier) stepped into the room. She said, "Jan, have you been waiting for me?" He smiled. And then his breathing stopped. I could sense his soul leaving his body. It was both extremely painful and beautiful. I am grateful that I got to be there with him as he transitioned. Yes, on a 9/11. Making sure I would never forget the date (as if I ever would).

My mum and I took a taxi home. She went to her place and I to mine. He told me instantly, "Do not cry. Do not upset the girls." They were staying with us that weekend but we went to his sister's house. She spotted that I was hurting.

"What's up?" she asked.

"My father died."

"Oh no, when?"

"Well, this afternoon," I said.

The look on her face.

She said, "Why are you here? Would you not rather be at home, or with your mum?"

She turned to her brother.

"Why don't you understand?" she said.

He replied, "Come on, her father had been sick for a while and he was old."

He did not allow me to grieve. Snapped at me when I cried. Was annoyed at the time that I spent on arranging the funeral. Did not support me when I got into huge fights with my brothers. Did not accompany me to the funeral. Whatever happened until then, whatever would happen after: not being able to grieve my father's death is what I hate him for the most.

Right after my father died, my mum was also diagnosed with cancer. A tumour very close to her kidneys. Luckily, it was discovered in time. On her birthday, in October, she got the results from the operation: all clear. I was in such a turmoil of emotions that I did not pay too much attention to the situation at home. Did not notice that he was moving towards physical violence. There was a lot of tension, the regular conflicts, the now standard name calling. He started to force me to partake in certain sexual actions that I did not fancy. To be 'open' for sex whenever he felt like it. But I did not see the first hit coming. But, it did. Soon and hard.

HIT HARD

He never took me dancing. But one night he said, "Do you

want to come with me to a salsa party in Utrecht." I said, "Sure!" I had always loved to dance. I had overcome my childhood shyness. I talked. Danced. Flirted. Had fun. At the party, we danced a few times. Some guys asked me to dance. I politely declined. He would have never accepted it. When he went to the toilet, I was at the bar ordering the drinks. A guy was standing next to me. Nice fellow, nothing more. We talked about salsa and Utrecht — regular stuff. When he came back and saw us talking, he went into a fit right there and then. I felt ashamed. Ashamed of the attention our fight was drawing. But also, at my 'behaviour'. He truly made me believe that I had behaved badly.

When driving back, he hit me in the face. Yes, in the car, whilst he was driving at high speed. It hurt me. It scared me. Could hardly believe what was happening. He hit me again. And again. Tried to open the door to throw me out, screaming and shouting. I was such a dirty whore. He had not even been gone for 5 minutes and I was seducing another guy. My mind was in overdrive. I could simply not process it all. By the time we got back to my house, I ran for the police station. They could not take my statement as it was late in the evening. Did I have a safe place to sleep? Yeah, I had. I went to my friend's house. I hardly slept a wink. As I was sitting there with a black and blue face, the news came in. Theo van Gogh, a very talented and thought-provoking Dutch filmmaker, had been murdered.

He had been dragged off his bike in broad daylight and stabbed to death by a radical Muslim. The news hit me even harder than it normally would have done. Another free soul silenced forever. Later that week I made a notification at the police station. Less heavy than pressing charges. It would make them get in contact with him though, to steer him towards counselling.

He wooed me again. Told me he would go to therapy. He loved me. The girls loved me. Oh, the girls... And, I was still processing so much stuff. My father's death. My mother's illness. I was so out of tune with myself. With everything. I was easily persuaded. Easily soothed. Easily fooled. To an outsider, it seems impossible that I would accept a guy hitting me. Any sane person would not. But I was anything but sane. I truly had no idea what to do.

Then he came up with this great plan. What if we were to spend New Year's Eve in Peru? Well, it would be a sort of a fresh start. I had always loved travelling. Had never been to Peru before. He would organise it all. A nice apartment, a trip to Machu Picchu. It would be marvellous. He travelled ahead to set it all up. I took the girls with me. It was a long trip, but we made it. When we got there, he had not arranged anything. The girls could stay with their mum's parents. I stayed with him in his old home for a few days in one of the poorest areas of Lima. A neighbourhood not visited by tourists. Small children started to cry when they saw me. With my fair complexion and red hair, I must have seemed an alien to them. When I would, however, start to speak Spanish, they lost their fear. After a few days, we rented an apartment in a fancy part of town. And when I say 'we' I mean 'I'. I paid for everything. I always paid for everything.

New Year's Eve. We had been invited by the girls' grandparents. He had dropped me and the girls off and had said, "I am just going to my old neighbourhood to see a few friends." 9pm. 10pm. 11pm. He was not there yet. Did not answer his phone. I got nervous. The girls got nervous. Their grandparents were ever so kind to me. They had seen him fuck up their daughter's life and were appalled that he was treating me in a similar shit manner. I was good to the girls, that they could see. They figured I deserved more respect. Midnight. Happy New Year... 10 past 12. He finally answered his phone. He clearly was with a woman. I think he showed up at around 3am. Drunk. The scent of a sweet perfume hanging all over him. His former in-laws were angry. He did not care. He never had cared. We never made it to Machu Picchu.

A few days later, it was time for all of us to go home together. On the way to the airport, he got angry — thinking that I had lost his sunglasses. Him going through all the luggage until he found them (yup somewhere where HE had put them) almost caused us to miss the flight. They did not have four seats in one row anymore. As I was a frequent traveller, I was placed in business class. He was outraged. Our first stopover was in Atlanta. We had to properly enter the USA. In the line up to the border security, he kept shouting at me. I came to the counter first. The officer said, "Madam, are you alright?" He had obviously noticed his behaviour. I said, "Yeah sure." Another angel sent my way. Another that I ignored.

At the second stopover, I tried to phone my mum. She did not answer. Did not think too much of it — she was always out and about. Once we finally made it to Schiphol, we took a taxi home. I switched on my mobile phone and I saw a great number of missed calls from my sister-in-law. I called her instantly. She told me my mum had been taken to hospital with a heart attack. Once at my place, he stayed there with the girls. I continued in the taxi to the hospital. My mum was okay — they had performed a small operation and she would recover fully. I, to date, wonder if all the tension in my relationship (mums know, they just do, even if you do not speak about it) had contributed to the attack. But my mum does not think so. Heart disease is common in her family. She lost most of her brothers and sisters to heart problems. Anyway, I was in shock again. Once again, he did not support me. He even tried to make me see my mum less regularly. In all fairness, I was so worried that she might notice that I was in a bad place, I did not stop by as much as I used to. The less (unspoken) questions, the better. All part of an abuser's master plan: isolate the prey. The more I felt alone, the more power he gained over me.

HIT ME BABY ONE MORE TIME

The year saw me undergoing physical violence more and more. For the seemingly weirdest of reasons. I recall he had once stood me up in a DIY store in the outskirts of town. No bus stop, no nothing. I however, by chance, had his phone in my purse. While I was sitting in the taxi (the only way to get home), I decided to have a little look inside. A shitload of texts to and from women that left nothing to the imagination. When I got home and confronted him, he beat me up. It was all my fault. I was such a bad woman, he had to seek comfort elsewhere. Another time I got home from work and he had been going through my bank statements. He hit me because he had discovered that I had lent funds to a platonic male friend. MY money. That I had earned. And that my friend had meanwhile paid back. But he thought I deserved to be punished. I fell silent more and more. Anything I said could trigger him. Anything could set him off.

More and more stories about women came to the surface. We were in a beach club and when he opened his wallet, I noticed a business card from a firm that I worked with regularly. He was not a corporate professional so why would he know this woman, who happened to be the assistant to one of my friends? He said he knew her from a salsa party. I replied, "Do you honestly think I want to sit at the same conference table with one of the women that you are doing on the side? If you fuck around, do not do it in my world." A world that was largely unaware of my relationship. And certainly, had no clue that I was being abused.

Then one of his other ladies thought she was pregnant. "If it turns out to be mine, can I bring the baby to our house?" You would think this would have woken me up. But I was in a totally different universe. If I was the most important woman in his life, I was okay with it. With anything. I had no self-respect left. There, alas, are many songs that make women believe that being someone's number one is good enough. I grew up with this narrative, as did many women. Well, if a guy is seeing a multitude of women, chances are that he is not good to any of them. He certainly was not good to me. Not in any way. He did not meet my emotional needs. Did not contribute financially. Never supported me. Violence manifests itself in so many ways — if it were just physical, it would be easier to spot and address. It is the sneaky mean little ways of them putting you down, that do you in. Day by day. That lady, she turned out not to be pregnant. One thing less to worry about.

YOU HAVE A FRIEND

I dreaded coming home after work. Work was my haven. I could be me there. I could laugh. I could be good at something. I could breathe. All the things I could not do anymore at home. It was so hard to lead a double life. For the outside world, I was the same professional, ever cheerful, go-getting lady. Showing up for work, doing the best I could — even more so than ever. For I could not afford to lose this job. He was not making any money. I showed up in the office every day. Covering up the scars — visible or not. Never showing my fears nor anxiety.

How I loved being in the office. Apart from the daily check-up phone calls and text messages from him, demanding to know what I was doing with whom and why, I could lean back in a bubble. In the 9 to 5 illusion, all was well. Nobody could see that I dreaded going home — even though I had to leave exactly on time in order not to upset him. Who would ever know that I was making that journey home each day with weak knees? Knowing that once I stepped through my front door, I had to let go of the very essence of me. That I would be expected to play a part in a play that was all but playful. I felt so ashamed. Who could I turn to? Who would believe me? Me, being beaten up at home. Really? I also dreaded advice like, "Leave now. Don't stand for this." For part of me knew that this was sound advice. A larger part of me had, however, already been so brainwashed that I simply could not walk away.

I was in luck. There were two people who always listened to me — also between the lines. Who were just there for me. Without judgement. One of them was a colleague who had become a dear friend. My coffee-buddy. Every morning we would meet up for coffee. Without ever uttering a word about the abuse, he could sense what I was facing, he provided daily comfort. He acknowledged me as a professional and as a person. Made me laugh. Allowed me to cry. He must have been wondering what was going on. I never asked if he knew, and sadly I cannot anymore. He died a few years ago — way too young from a mere human perspective. The other was a long-standing friend who had undergone abuse in many forms herself. She got it. She got me. Was always there for me when I reached out to her. Never ever judged me. Never ever forced me to leave. Day or night, I could call her or take a taxi to her house. Stay for as long as I wished. Those two marvellous people, I can honestly say, have helped me make it through it all.

CHRISTMAS EVE

Jingle bells... the restaurant at my favourite seaside restaurant was filled with couples celebrating Christmas

Eve. Lovely food, Christmas music, what could possibly go wrong? Well, with him, anything and everything. As usual. I cannot remember what the fight was about. But I recall that he left me there without any money. He had taken my wallet from me. There I was, far from home. I did have my phone. Not willing to risk a public transport fine, after all I was already stressed out, I called a friend. Her boyfriend came to the rescue and brought me home. He was there. He had cooled down. We went to his sister's. The night was not holy. Silent, yes that I was.

A BRAZILIAN

A Brazilian. Not of the waxing kind. Albeit it did rip me apart on many levels. An all you can eat shrimp buffet and all you can drink caipirinhas jar-fest led to a near death experience. Intoxicated? Yes. Hung over? Hung up...

After the Christmas Eve disaster, I had gotten rid of him. Again. This time for good. Aided by my best friend's boyfriend who threw him and his stuff out, both my house and my agenda were empty. When my best friend said, "Join us in Brazil." I thought, "Sure!" New Year's Eve. Celebrated in a plane whilst crossing the Atlantic. Landed jet lagged, but that did not stop me from joining the party squad to an all you can eat shrimp buffet. A few shrimps later, we moved on to the bar next door. All night party hour, caipirinhas by the jar. On my way to the loo, a very handsome Brazilian started to talk to me. Explaining that he just had to kiss me as I to him was a gorgeous woman. Priorities, however, saw me running to the toilet and onwards to the hotel before his lips could touch mine. That this non-kiss would be a very dear one, I could not foresee.

When I got back to Amsterdam, he was waiting for me. He was ever so sorry. Yada, yada. He wanted me back, even though I no doubt had behaved like a white whore in Brazil. I told him that I did not even kiss a guy when I had the chance.

Life continued, as usual. He did not work (much), he expected me to do everything in the house. If even one detail was not to his liking, he would lash out. Verbally but also physically. Details such as: not buttering the sandwiches properly. I got more tense and sad and lonely as time progressed. Did not go out with my friends. Did not even call them when I was in the house. Saw my mother less and less. Could not randomly send emails — he would check my email box every single day. It was like being the main character in *Enemy of the State*. To isolate me even further, he suggested we move to the countryside. We did. I had not driven a car since coming back from Curaçao and had developed a fear of driving. I was properly stuck in that house. The nearest train station was a 25-minute walk. There I was, a city girl in the middle of nowhere. And it was nothing like *The Good Life*.

EEEEK-R

"Do you know where you are?" the nurse asked me.

"I do. I am at the Slotervaart Hospital. But, if I would not have known, I could have fooled you by reading out the sign on the wall there."

"Okay fair enough, do you know which street we are in?"

"Sure, I do. Johan Huizinga Lane."

The nurse looked at me puzzled, a wobbly smile on his face.

I said, "You do not know, do you? Nope, I am from a different province." Oops, another cognitive test, failed by him.

Twenty-four hours earlier...

It had been a regular Sunday night. He would bring the girls back to their mother, go out to a salsa party and have sex with other women. I would clean the house and worry. Worry about what he was up to and with whom and if he would come home. Also, oh the irony, worried that he would come home. Drunk. Angry. Doomed if he would, doomed if he would not ...

He got home just after midnight. He was in a foul mood. I decided to let him be and sleep in the girls' room. I could hear him come upstairs and thought he had fallen asleep. Whether he did sleep or not, I will never know. What I do know is that I was awakened rudely. He threw the door open, dragged me off the bed and started screaming, shouting, and hitting me. Usually there was a build up to physical violence. Name calling. His voice rising. Tension building up to an explosion. Not this night. He just lashed out. To my body. To my face. All over. In between hitting me, he kept shouting that I did have sex with that guy in Brazil. That I had betrayed him. That I was a Dutch whore, a slut, a devil, a dirty woman, not worth a penny. How had I dared disrespect him? How many more men had I slept with? I could not be trusted. I should suffer. Suffer hard.

He had been violent many times before. But this time it was different. I saw evil in his eyes. The brute, dark, destructive force of evil. A force that lies in all of us. But that most of us manage to control. Even in violent situations. In all the previous attacks, he had been in control. Hurting me badly, but still fully in control of the situation. Not this night. He allowed evil to take over. And evil, dear readers, is deadly. It will stop at nothing. Has no sense of humanity, compassion, love nor kindness. It sets out to kill. Destruct. He was a knowing and willing vessel.

Fully conscious of and fully responsible for his actions. By being who he was, by doing what he had done for so long to me and so many women before me, he had set himself up for a moment in which he would give in to the evil inside of himself. Which would make him 100 per cent able and willing to kill. And he was. He was ever so ready. To seek my blood. To drag my soul out of my body. He wanted me dead. Right there and then.

Usually a physical attack would last about 10 minutes. When those minutes had passed and he kept hitting and kicking me, I got scared. Scared on an unknown level. I had been afraid, anxious, worried, frightened a zillion times before — about so many things, not just in this relationship. There had been so many scary moments in my life. My parents splitting up. The bullying at school. The guys who had toyed with me — emotionally, not physically. But never had I been as afraid as I was then. There was blood running down my face. Blood running from my mouth. Not a body part was untouched. He kept hitting and kicking me everywhere. And the shouting. He kept screaming at me. In Dutch. In Spanish. My mind was in overdrive and the worst part was that I felt like I had deserved it. I had been a bad girlfriend. I had been too loose with men before meeting him. I had wanted to kiss the guy in Brazil. But I had not kissed him. And even if I had done so, we were not together at that time. But he was right, it had been wrong of me. So wrong. I was evil. I deserved to suffer.

I felt myself slipping — the pain got too much. Mentally and physically. Who was I? Where was I? What the hell was happening? I had hardly any strength left to counter his attack. To defend myself. To beg him to stop. For I had tried to make him see sense. I had tried to explain why he should STOP. That he would end up killing me. He did not stop. Not for a second.

Then his hands reached for my throat.

I found myself in a most wonderful, peaceful place. There was only peace and quiet. The most radiant blue light. A sense of calmness. Of belonging. Of home. Of being safe. I had never felt happier. More complete. It was bliss. Just 100 per cent bliss. Oh, how I had longed for this place. I had never truly grounded on earth. Had always been restless. Had always sensed there was something more. A sanctuary where my soul could rest. I was there now. I felt as light as a feather. Floating. Oh, the joy...

Then I encountered the second rude awakening of that evening. I woke up. Or, as I still see it, I was thrown back into my body. Into my human format. Never ever have I been angrier. I had been so happy there. That anger of being back was so great that it took me a while to notice that he was still hitting me. I had passed out (or more accurately I had died). But he was still at it. I tried to tell him that I had passed out. That I had almost died. He suddenly stopped. And said, "Let's go in the bathroom, so you can clean yourself up a bit." I thought, "Okay, this is it. It is over. It will all be okay now." That is how it had always ended. We would fight. Verbally. He would start hitting me. He would stop. He would be sorry. I had no reason to assume that this time would be different.

We went into the bathroom. He handed me a towel. I looked at myself in the mirror above the sink. It was a scary sight. Black and blue — the deepest of black and blue imaginable. Blood flowing. Blood already drying up. After a minute or so, however, I saw the look in his eyes changing again.

His job was not done.

His need to kill me was still there.

He ripped the towel from my hands and when he hit me again, I thought, "I will die. And not return. I will not survive this." The sun came up — a sign that the attack had already lasted for six hours. I threw up. The pain was just too much. Okay then, let me go back to where I had just been. To the happy place. Where I would be free. Every cell in my body was ready to make that transition (again). Then, however, he stopped. HE JUST STOPPED. I could not believe it. I was ready for the violence to resume. He did seem very tired though. Said, "Let's go to sleep. When we wake up, I will take you to a doctor. You can tell them that you had an accident in the bathroom. It will be okay."

He loved me. He forgave me. We would be happy together, forever. Now, sleep.

We went to the bedroom. He passed out. I was wide awake. Adrenaline rushing. Survival mode had kicked in. I had a chance now. A chance to escape. If he kept asleep. For if he would wake up whilst I did a runner, that would be the end of it. The end of me. I started to calculate. So many steps to the bedroom door. So many down the hall. Down the stairs. To the hall downstairs. Where was my coat? Where was my phone? Where was my bag? I calculated each and every step. Each and every second. Over and over again. By his breathing, I could tell that he was fast asleep. I took a deep breath and started to walk. For doing a runner it was not, I could hardly walk. Down that hall. Down the stairs. Found my things downstairs. Kissed the cat goodbye. Opened the door. Made it to the end of the driveway. Turned right. I was not going to the train station. If he would wake up, he would seek me there. I went the other way.

Then I remembered: I had a dentist appointment that morning. I called the dentist. Called my office — so sorry, I had fallen in the bathroom, I was going to see a doctor.

Kept walking. My nephew lived close by. I called his wife. She came searching for me. I had said, "Please do not take me to a doctor." But she was adamant that I needed medical care. "Let's go to the ER. Afterwards we can go to my house." I begged her not to tell my brother (her father-in-law), nor my mum. She said, "No, I will not call them."

We went into the ER. It was a Monday morning, not that many people waiting. When my niece told them that I had been beaten and strangled to the point that I had passed out, I was immediately put into a hospital bed and taken to the neurology department. I will never forget the compassion in the neurologist's eyes — he cared, he truly did. It was decided that I had to stay in the hospital for at least 24 hours. They wanted to run hourly tests. Ensuring that I did not have a concussion or other brain damage. They ran some x-rays, which showed that he had broken three of my ribs. There was not a bone in my body that was not hurting. Everything was black and blue — around my throat, you could see his fingerprints. He had made his mark, in so many ways. It was a sheer miracle that I had not died of strangulation.

My nephew's wife did not keep her promise of not telling my brother and mother. She was right. They needed to know. Of all that happened during this hellish night, nothing was worse than seeing the look on my mother's face when she saw me in that hospital bed. I will never forgive him, nor myself, for having made her go through this. No mother should ever find her child in such a situation. It is just too hard to bear. My brothers were there. They were mad. My youngest brother wanted to beat him up as badly he had done me. Or send the police to the house. They urged me to press charges against him. I stopped them. Because there was something in that house that I did not want anybody to know about. Nor did I wish for my brother or any family member to get into trouble with the law over him — he simply was not worth it. After an hour or so, they left. I had expected them to return later, with some clothing perhaps. For I had nothing other than the blood-stained clothes I'd arrived in. The smelly bloody clothes. Sweat caused by fear smells awful. I recall that smell vividly. But none of them came back to visit me. There I was. Alone. Apart from the medical staff that had to wake me up every hour. Who were amazed at my resilience. At my sense of humour through it all. Humour saw me through... again. This was it; you may think. This was the end of this relationship. The end of this story. Alas, it was not.

THE THINGS WE LOST IN THE FIRE

I had returned to him. Not just like that. I was hurt, on so many levels. Scared. But he had a grip on me. Not just from a love perspective. He had been getting himself in all sorts of trouble. And me knowing about it could be detrimental to my career. Not that I approved of any of his plans. He had forced this shit upon us. But here he was. Here I was. I knew that he could turn any story his way. That he could make me, make the world, believe all sorts. That he could destroy my reputation. The fear of losing everything was greater than the fear of potentially being killed again. I had not pressed charges. I had wanted him to get help — time in prison would not have changed his mindset towards me or other women. Now I just wished for him to make the money that he had his eyes on so we could split up and I could return to my normal life. It was awkward living in that house again. The house in which I had nearly lost my life. I told him, "This place is tainted by evil energy. It needs to be cleansed." But whereas sage might have done the trick, nothing cleanses like... fire.

We had rented the house from a family that went to live abroad. And by 'we' I mean 'I'. I had rented the house. My name was on the lease. One day, late afternoon, we had been to a DIY shop and were driving towards the house. A family member of the lessors called me. When I answered, I could hear the panic in his voice. "Sandra, the house is one fire!"

My heart skipped a beat or two. You see, he had always

thought of himself as a skilled electrician. I had, however, doubted his abilities. And, here we had it: total disaster. We went straight to the house. My mind in total overdrive. When we arrived, there were firefighters and, of course, also the police. Luckily, the cat was okay. They took us in for questioning. I was granted the infamous one phone call. I called my colleague — my coffee buddy. He was not there but I put on his voicemail, "Could you tell HR that I am ill?" The policemen were kind and considerate. It soon became apparent, aided by the hospital reports of the attack, that I had been under a lot of undue pressure and could not be held accountable for his stupidity that had led to the fire. But they could not keep him in custody for much longer. As devastating as causing a house fire is, it has its limitations when it comes to keeping him in jail for longer than a day or so. If I would, however, now give a statement on the attempted murder, he would not be out for a long time. So, I did.

When I was released, I sincerely contemplated drowning myself in the sea. As I was looking for a bus stop to take me to the beach, my friend Jo called. One of my always-there friends. She managed to talk me out of my plan and said, "Come and stay with me. It may seem hopeless now, but you will make it through. I know you will."

He stayed in jail for a little over six months. During that time, I dealt with the civil law repercussions of the damage. My name had been on the lease and the house insurance did not cover all costs to rebuild the house. I made up the difference in hefty monthly instalments. Ten years it took me to pay them back. To date, I feel guilty towards that family. I know the situation I was in. They knew too. Not just by having read the police reports. In the garden shed they had found my emergency bag. Upon returning, I had hidden some cash, clothes, keys, and paperwork. Just in case. Did I have a choice back then? Telling on him would have cost me a lot. At least my job. Most probably also my life. But still. I shall never forgive myself.

LIGHTBULB

Then, as I had been totally brainwashed for so many years, I started to feel guilty for having put him in jail. When he got out, he made sure to turn up that guilt-volume. How could I have put him there? But he had been working with a psychologist and had calmed down so much. He forgave me (no, this is not a typo …. he was so kind as to forgive me). The girls had missed me. All would be good. It was seemingly alright at first. I had not told a soul about this unholy reunion, knowing what kind of reaction I would receive from family and friends. There was a bit of tension for sure. But no violence.

Spring 2007. A few weeks into the New Us. We were sitting on the sofa. His youngest daughter was with us that weekend. Saturday night. We zapped into a movie about a woman who, thinking she was terminally ill, visits a swank resort that she had always dreamed about. Swank the resort was. Truly fancy. Lavish buffets. Grandeur beyond compare. Suddenly he said to me, "If our lives improve, we should go to a resort like this." And then it clicked. FINALLY, it clicked. There it was. The lightbulb of all lightbulbs. An AHA to the moon and back. I thought, "If I stay with you, I will never ever have a chance to improve my life. To do anything really. Anything but be miserable, sad, isolated. This is it. You have got to go." I felt so calm. Not a shadow of doubt. I was free. It had taken me too long. Cost me too much. But now I was free again.

I did not want to upset his daughter by chucking them both out late in the evening, so my plan was to wait until he brought her home tomorrow evening and goes out on the town. I would then pack his bags and that would be the end of it. The next day, we went to his sister's house. She lived out of town in a small village. His sister was in the kitchen cooking. His daughter was watching a movie. He was on the other side of the living room. His phone rang. He answered in Spanish. Even though by then I spoke Spanish fluently, even with his family, he and I had always spoken in Dutch. As if he did not know that I could understand him, he agreed to a date with the caller (obviously a woman) for that same evening. Whilst he looked chuffed with himself, I searched for his jacket in the hallway and from his keyring, I took the keys to my apartment. When he was done with his call, I asked him to step outside for a minute. There I told him, "Right, this evening at 9pm your stuff will be on the sideway next to the door. Collect it or otherwise the garbage van will take it with them in the morning." He thought I was joking. After all we had been through, certainly I would not... I walked away. Towards the bus stop. As I approached, there it was, the once an hour bus to Amsterdam. Freedom. Once home, I collected this stuff. He did collect it all. To both his and my surprise, that truly was the end of it. He tried to call. I did not respond anymore. Game over.

RECAP: It did not click when he cheated on me. It did not click when he started to hit me. It did not click when he tried to kill me. It did not click when I ended up with a huge debt. It clicked at a seemingly random moment. Because of one remark. To this day, I am thankful that we zapped into that movie. The main character, by the way, ended up not being terminal. She lived on. And finally, so did I.

What I, however, failed to do was heal from this experience. I did not process it. Did not address the vulnerabilities that had gotten me into this mess. Did not learn how to set boundaries. Which lead to another nasty relationship. Enter... the third HIM.

Him Number 3
THE ADDICT

DANCE INTO SEDUCTION

November 2007. I had made it through the working day. After a short or, depending on how you view it, long night. Before going home to get some well needed sleep, my colleagues dragged me to a farewell party for our HR lady. I drank, made some suggestive remarks about last night that cracked up my coffee buddy. Drank some more. After all, best fight fire (hangover) with fire (more drinks). Survived the tram journey and put the keys in the door, expecting to land into an empty house. But to my surprise, there he was. The guy from the night before. An intentional one-night stand who turned himself into a one-night stay. He was sitting on the sofa watching the Spanish

TV channel, and said, "Would you like a cuppa? And, when you are warmed up a bit, let's go to the supermarket and then I will cook dinner." I thought, "Okay, why not turn it into a two-night stand? Surely that would be fine. After all, he would shortly be off to Barcelona. One more night."

Tuesday evening, two days before. To squeeze as much after work activities into a week as possible, I rushed from my Spanish lesson to my salsa class. I had known the salsa teacher like forever. He could not teach me anything new but was happy for me to dance along. Usually I partnered up with the more experienced dancers. Yet, this evening there was a newbie in our advanced class. Would I?.... not really but okay. The guy was as advanced in salsa as I am in Japanese (hint: I can count to ten in Japanese due to years of karate training. but that is sort of it — sushi aside). Kept stepping on my toes. Had no rhythm. Yet, he was convinced that he was the Fred Astaire of the salsa world and even suggested that I was out of beat. That was IT. I snapped. Ran off the dancefloor and before heading down the stairs, I shouted in Spanish to the teacher and his mistress (official title: assistant but hey, we all knew) in plain Cuban that I was done with his kind of imbeciles. I pay for advanced, so bring me advanced!

The next day the salsa teacher called me. I was right. Would I please, please return to class? I could pick my dance partners in class, whatever would make me happy. "And please join me for a drink after the Thursday class so we can dance, drink and make-up." That Thursday I ran from a church meeting (yes, it was a sort of Maria turns into Maria Magdalena transition) to a bar near the salsa school. The teacher was already there with a group of students. I sat down and poured down a few margaritas to warm me up from the pouring rain outside. Danced with the teacher. Then a guy joined our table. He seemed to know the teacher.

"Do you dance?" he asked in English and with a smile.

"Yes."

"Salsa?"

"Yes."

"Bachata?"

"Well I do, but I am not really into it."

"Would you give it a try with me?"

"Sure."

We had a great click on the dance floor (you can see a theme emerging here: dance well with me and I will easily forgive you all kinds of shit). This is not a matter of experience; it is all about energy. To this day, there are advanced dancers that I cannot dance with. But he and I, we worked. Rather well. He did not realise that I spoke Spanish until he asked the teacher whether he was doing me. And I responded, "NO, he is too busy with this and that lady on the other side of the bar." The look on his face, priceless. He was Cuban, like the teacher, and lived around the corner from the bar. He had stopped by that evening because he was heading to Barcelona soon and wanted to say goodbye to his friends.

After a few more rounds of salsa and drinks, the bar was almost closing. He had suggested we move on to a Latin bar at the Leidseplein, but I was not sure. It was already rather late. He said, "Wait for me, I must go to the bathroom." And I vividly recall thinking, "Why bother? I should just go home." But I waited. That inkling (intuition, universe calling), I go back to that moment often. What if?... We went to that Latin bar. It seemed so normal to take him home. It had been a while and I knew that if the click is there on the dancefloor, it will work well in bed too. It did. I may have slept for an hour or so. Left for the office and said to him, "Just close the door behind you when you go." Well, he did not.

Saturday evening. Usually I went to my mums on a Saturday afternoon. We would shop a bit and then I would have dinner there. He rang me. He was in a Spanish restaurant; wanted to know if I would like to join. "Oh, you have eaten already. Desert then?" Why not. Un, dos, tres, noches... He was the light of the party at the restaurant. I devoured my crema catalana and sipped on some sweet white wine. By chance, a salsa party was on close by. We went there and he sort of introduced me to his friends as his girlfriend. Which I know, is a very fluid definition — it ranges from I have just done her in the toilet and cannot recall her name to 'we have been together for 20 years and we have three kids'. Girlfriend? Well, the jury was still out on that one. We had fun – something I had lacked for a long time — but he was heading for Barcelona and I was happy being single. Lots of plans on the horizon. Advanced Spanish courses in Sevilla and Buenos Aires. Emigrating again at some point. But I did like him caring for me in a very hands-on manner. The cups of tea, cooking me dinner, asking how I was. Normal things but as I came from the dark trenches of an abusive relationship, I perceived this kind of attention as being seen, as being valued.

Sunday moved into Tuesday. I did not know exactly when he was heading for Barcelona. Had not asked because up to that point, I had not cared. That evening someone called him. A girl. Angry. They spoke in Spanish. Is it not funny that even though he and I had now been speaking Spanish for days, he still did not get that I would understand so clearly what this conversation was about? From what I could hear, she was pissed because he had not arrived in

Barcelona that afternoon. She had paid for his ticket. So, what was the deal? He tried to calm her down. When he put down the phone and tried to convince me that she was just a friend, I told him, "If you are staying here, I never ever want to be party to such a phone call. Had enough of those in my relationship journey." So there and then, he chose to stay. And I chose to believe in a happy ending. This time, it would all go well. I bypassed the facts that he did not have a home in the Netherlands, nor a job. Plus, he had badly stood up a girl in Barcelona who had paid for his ticket. How easily we deceive ourselves for a bit of attention. I was fair game to him. Easy game. The game did not end there, alas. That evening we went to a party hosted by the salsa teacher. He was surprised to see us together and said to him in Spanish, "You are a shark." I thought it was just a joke. As it turned out, the joke was on me.

SNIFF SNIFF

Another crazy night. He had cooked. We drank, danced in the living room, made love. Then he said, "Damn, I am out of cigarettes and even the night shop is closed now."

"Well there are bars nearby, probably they would sell them there."

"No, I know this guy who will stop by. Will you lend me 50 euro?"

"Hmmm, that is a lot of money for cigarettes."

But I was love-drunk and tired up to a point of collapsing after a fortnight of fun whilst still working the nine to five. A fellow did stop by. Shortly, he was all cheerful again after having been extremely restless. In hindsight, I could have seen it. Should have seen it. But in my 38 years in Amsterdam, I knew nobody who did cocaine. Alcohol addicts, for sure. And the second him had later said that he had attacked me so furiously that near fatal night because of a one-time coke-try. Yet regular use, nope, I did not recognise the signs. Not then anyway. Later I saw it. In this him. In my memories of the second him. In people at work. In people on the TV. It turned out that they knew each other, the abuser and the addict. Not only because they had been going to the same salsa parties. They had also shared the same dealer. The addict never knew of my existence, as the abuser never took me dancing. When I had told him about the abuser he had said, "I think I know this geezer. Do you have a picture?" Yup, it was him alright. The addict had even sat in our car. Small world.

DAY AND NIGHT

Day and night, night and day. Not only were our personalities totally different, we also differed when it came to when we lived and worked. I would get up at 5:30am, be at the office at 6:15am, worked an hour, went to the gym, continued working until 5:30pm and would then venture home. He would get up at around 4pm, cook a bit and before I got home, would head off to the restaurant or bar that he would work at that week. He changed employers often, blaming it all on the restaurants, of course. They did not want to keep staff on for long, the managers were liars, the clients were too difficult to deal with — no doubt '1000 lies to tell your spouse' was his favourite google search. Work to me was a way to make ends meet, which was getting harder and harder given his costly addiction. Work to him was an excuse to be at The Place to Be: the Amsterdam nightlife where bars closed late, and dealers were at hand (well, he did save mobile phone fees this way).

Not once did he venture home directly after work. He went from bar to bar, often entering the house long after I had gone off to work. If at all. I recall a Saturday or Sunday morning, 11am-ish. He had not come home, again. My mum stopped by and then he entered. I made up some lame excuse about him having helped a friend. I made up lame excuses all the time. I did not want the world to know that yes, once again, I had fallen for a totally useless idiot who was eating me alive.

With the first and second him, I had gotten accustomed to guys staying out late. Until the next morning even. This him, however, added a curious plot twist to my regular 'worried sick routine'. Like on most nights, we had dinner and we had a few drinks. He a few more than me. I would venture to bed around 11pm as I had to get up early for work. He would then watch telenovelas on the internet or listen to music. He usually crashed on the sofa downstairs. When I woke up around 3am — I have not once in my life slept for 8 hours straight — I went to look for him. He was not there. I panicked. Called his cell phone. Repeatedly. No reply. I checked my online banking. I had given him access to one of my accounts. I could see that he had withdrawn cash to the maximum credit amount — around 700 euros in total. What the fuck? Where was he? He would at times say that he was no use to anybody (in hindsight, I would say that is correct) and that he had better leave me. Leave the Netherlands all together. I thought that he had done a runner. I went to the office and at around 1 pm or so he called me. Stoned, drunk, disorientated. Yeah, a mate had called him, and he had gone looking for him in town and then they had gone to an all night after night 24/7 Latin bar. Where he had fallen asleep on the floor. I was angry. And pleased that he was well. He was ever so sorry...

Like a true vampire who could not handle the light, he ate away at my money, my time, and my energy. After the first love-struck months, I started to see through him — and I had wanted OUT a great number of times. It would take the birth of my son to let go of him forever. But before I had my son, I married him. It would be my second wedding. Had never intended to get married again. I had arranged for my Catholic marriage to be annulled, which had been a long and intensive process, solely to grant my ex-husband the opportunity to get married in church again. But he had popped the question a few weeks after we had met. And I had said yes. Yes, to what actually? To what I thought was a dream. To what turned out to be a nightmare.

HIS PAPERS, MY WORK

When we had first met, he had given the impression that he was done with the Netherlands, which is why he had planned to go to Spain. The Netherlands, however, seemed to be done with him. He did not have a permit anymore and had hoped that he could obtain Spanish nationality if he would move there. The girl from Spain that he had been fighting with over the phone had met him by chance on a trip to Amsterdam. He had wooed her to the extent that she had bought him a bus ticket to Spain where she would look after him. I guess that last minute, I turned out to be the bigger fish.

Well, if he was going to stay here, we needed to sort out a permit. Had this been the reason for his impromptu wedding proposal? I did wonder. But I also wanted to believe that he truly felt for me. When I took him to a solicitor, a pleasant surprise awaited us. As he did not have a registered address, the Dutch government had not been able to find him. They had contacted his former solicitor as he was awarded a permit based on having a daughter in the Netherlands. However, the solicitor could not find him either — until I had dragged him there to restart the proceedings. It did cost me a lot of money to pay the outstanding permit/solicitor fees. But at least now he had a legal title. He could work. And, WOW, he still wanted to marry me. Now I knew for sure: he loved me. Me! Not my money. Not my nationality. Me.

THE RUN UP TO THE WEDDING

In the Netherlands, a church wedding does not include a civil registration. Either you just get married in a civil ceremony (which can take place at lots of lovely places) or you first go civil and then onwards to a church ceremony. We had opted for a civil wedding on a Monday and then the church wedding on Saturday. He had not seen his parents for eight years so I left no stone unturned to arrange a reunion. It cost me a lot of money in permit fees and plane tickets, but I managed to bring them to the Netherlands. His mum was omnipresent. If he were to step into the bathroom, she would wait for him in the hallway. Same for the fridge — imagine someone walking with you to the fridge, standing there whilst you search for your food (in his case, drink ...). She would sit next to him on the sofa and rub his feet as if he were a baby — all the time. As a Cuban friend who grew up in the same neighbourhood as him would say, "Even for a Cuban mum, she is extreme."

The lack of privacy combined with a growing sense that I was making a huge mistake, again, did not provide for a merry pre-marriage atmosphere. I was on edge, or rather over the edge already. I had begged him not to use cocaine on the night before the wedding. Saying 'I do' seemed like a decision best taken sober. But one of his female Cuban friends, whom he had slipped in as a wedding witness last minute, came around and whilst I was trying to get some sleep, they partied like there was no tomorrow. Tomorrow did come, however. I could hardly contain my anger when I saw his bloodshot eyes. Gosh, did you not see the universe warning you big time? Again? Oh, I did. But I was on the wedding train. The 'Let me show the world that there is a good guy who wants me' train. A train that could had been featured in the World's Worst Commutes – it proved to be a one-way ticket to misery.

My mum and best friend arrived at around 8am. The ceremony would be at 9 o'clock, free of charge. It would be a dear occasion though in so many ways. They noticed how stressed out I was. But hey, aren't all brides? Even second chance brides. After we had dressed up (casual white jeans, saving the dress for church) we walked to the city hall. His female friend was claiming centre stage, as usual. She was very loud and made her presence well and truly known. Even more so when high. My anger spiralled. The ceremony was short and sweet. Notwithstanding that it was free, the civil servant did her utmost to make it special for us. For him, it was clearly a show. He was more bothered with his parents and friend than with me.

THE UNCIVIL WEDDING

The ceremony lasted just 15-minutes. I had not even spoken to him apart from to say 'I do'. His friend kept claiming his attention. She called her daughter and pushed the phone in my face — the daughter wanted to congratulate me. I was not up for that. The reality of it all had hit me. There I was, married to a coke addict who could not care less about me. He was only paying attention to his parents and friend. All I wanted was OUT. I recall saying to myself, "Wow, you beat Britney Spears. Her shortest marriage lasted a day or so. Yours just 15-minutes...."

I pushed the phone back at the friend, which caused her to shout and scream at me. Back at the house, the situation exploded even further. I unleashed all the hurt and anger. In no uncertain words. He took his friend's side and they left the house together. There I was. With the in-laws, my mum, and my bestie. I called at the neighbours' houses, explaining that the small party we had planned for that evening had been cancelled. He called his family and they left to wherever he had gone. I sent my mum and friend home. I can only imagine how helpless they must have felt. Being a mum now myself, I cannot imagine seeing my son going through similar hurt without being able to truly reach him.

I walked the streets in despair. Finally, I caught up with my new husband and his friend. They were drinking and being jolly at a bar, as if nothing had happened. And to them, it had not. After all, I was the nutter — the Dutch idiot who did not understand them. Here my memory fails me. Did I sit down with them or did we all go home together? Did I walk past or did they show up at some point? It is all a bit of a blur. Eventually we kissed and made up. He forgave me...

TAKE ME FROM THE CHURCH, AND FAST...

Fast forward to the church wedding. The night before, we had a huge row again. I was running around like a headless chicken (seemingly on speed, but that was not me, that was him). So many last-minute things to take care of (decorations for the restaurant, flowers, check on transport). Whilst I was on this organisational marathon, he called. He and his folks were hungry. Did I tell him to just get food? Nope. I ordered a Chinese takeaway and dropped that off at the house. By drop, I do mean drop. I threw it on the table, consumed by anger. He started to shout at me. I ran out. Off to my mum's, where I would spend the night.

When I woke up the next morning, I had no idea if he would show up at the church. I got dressed — the dress looked a lot lovelier than I did. I took a taxi to the hairdressers, conveniently located next to the church. My godfather appeared. He was totally unaware of all the turmoil and did a great job at keeping me sane.

Then he called.

Why had I not called him all day? The coach I had hired for all the wedding guests was late and… and….

All that came to mind, were scenes from *Runaway Bride*.

Yet I was already hooked in the eyes of the law. I put on the veil and a fake smile and played the part of the happy bride. The ceremony was wonderful. The dean was also a dear friend, and his warm and loving words did calm me down. We exchanged rings – the rings that my parents had once worn. He was standing there, in my church, with my father's ring on his finger, telling me lies. Telling us all lies.

After the ceremony, he and I took a water taxi to the restaurant. These were the only minutes that we were alone that day. Right before arriving at the restaurant, rain started to pour down. Torrential rain. Said to be a sign of good luck. Hmmm. That luck ran out soon. When we entered the restaurant, my family and friends were quietly having a drink. As is customary, they had waited for us to arrive to open the buffet. The Cubans, however, had taken over the place. Shouting, dancing, eating... He ignored my guests and sat down with his lot. And that was the last that I saw of him that evening. There is not one picture of us together at that party. Not one. Not even one dance. One kiss. One 'I Love You'. He was on a high, properly. Literally. In his circles, you did not bring flowers or gifts to a party. You brought drugs. He feasted on those. Big time.

WEDDED AND WEEPING

I had fun with my friends and family. To a certain extent. Some knew that I was not happy. Others sensed it. It was a weird night in many ways. The party ended at midnight and we headed to the hotel next to the restaurant. All close to our house, where a sort of after party was going on. He was too high to sleep (or anything ...). At around 5am, some of his friends started to shout his name in front of the hotel. Charming... I did not sleep a lot that night. He fell asleep at 8am and I made my way down to the hotel restaurant for breakfast. I could feel the staff thinking, "Where is the groom?" There I was. Alone. Again. There is nothing worse than being lonely whilst in a relationship. Especially on your wedding day and night. What had we said Yes, I Do to? For him, it was convenience (a woman who organised and paid for everything) and a chance to shine in front of his family and friends. For me, it was a desperate attempt to leave a dark history behind. To be able to say, "Yes, I am with somebody." But ultimately, I had only gained a liability. It was a huge 'No, I Do Not Love Myself Enough' statement. This him may not have hit me physically but emotionally it was as bad to be with this him as it had been with the second him.

THE MAKING OF MY SON

A son. I had never wanted kids. Not having had the most balanced childhood myself, I did not feel like I should put another human being on this planet. What if (s)he would be bullied, just like me? What if (s)he would grow up in a broken family too? Add to it the remarks made by my mum, "You should never have a child. You are just as selfish as your dad." NOW, I can see that she was projecting too much onto me. That she was trying to protect me. But it did make a huge imprint on me. Having a child was not on my agenda.

My first marriage came and went — neither of us had wished to have children at that stage. Relationships followed in which I became a sort of stepmother. The abusive him had said often, "I would never want to have a kid with you, I do not want my child to have your devilish blood." Then along came this him. On our first evening together, he had mentioned that he had two children. He was not in contact with them, but he did seem to care about them. When a few months later he started to say, "I would like to have a child with you," I started to think, "Hmmm. Maybe that would be a way to not lose his children (assuming contact would be established at some point) if we were to break up." That had happened a few times and it had caused me great grief.

I grew into the idea. Had my IUD removed, and the waiting game began. Period after period, hurt after hurt. We may have succeeded earlier IF he had made love to me often. But apart from us hardly ever being together, he preferred to watch adult movies (I am not shy of the P word but let's make it easier on the publishing platforms to brand this novel) whilst being high. Yes, this relationship surely was another great confidence booster! Eventually we went to Cuba for three weeks. More fun and games time. We returned. As did my period. I gave up on the idea. He had also shown me during this trip that he would never be structured enough to be a good husband, let alone father. Meanwhile there was a lot of unrest in the group I was managing at the office. Senior management vowed to back me up but they ended up stabbing me in the back.

During those weeks, I felt tired and sick. Burnout came to mind. I called in sick, found myself a lawyer, burn out coach, job coach, the works. Both I and my employer were heading towards a semi-amicable solution. Then my friend, who had a similar menstrual cycle as I did, told me that her period had come. Mine had not. Oh well, I thought, must be the stress. Days went by. One Tuesday morning, I decided to get a test. Just in case. I was at the drugstore at 8am. At 8:15 am, I took the test in the upstairs bathroom. Dingdong pregnant. I was so happy. Surprised and happy. I vividly recall walking down the stairs whilst shouting, "Look! Look! I am pregnant!" The way he looked at me is still in the top five worst moments of my life (which, given my previous experiences with toxic men, is a tough spot to hit). It was the most disgusted look ever. He was not pleased at all and went off to bed. I made it through the day with very mixed feelings.

That evening, my best friend and the dean who married us came to dinner. They were the first people I told about my pregnancy and they were very pleased. He pretended to be though. After having done a few more tests, just to be sure, I got myself together and went to work, that is: went to work on getting back to work. For this was NOT the time to switch jobs. With the help of my GP and a lawyer, I squared it at the office. What would follow were tough and lonely months.

A CAESAREAN AND A CUT THROUGH THE HEART

The pregnancy had not been without complications. I suffered from nausea for months. He had not changed his ways. Out and about every single night. I was facing it all by myself. Three times I started to bleed. The first time in an early stage. When I was on the toilet, I saw blood. I freaked out. Called the doctor. I went straight from the office to the hospital, which was close by. Had not even thought about waking him up to accompany me. Luckily, it turned out to be just a bladder infection. The second time, I was in my 26th week. It was a Sunday afternoon. He was still asleep. Again, I did not wake him up. The thought of him, still stoned like a skunk, coming with me to the hospital was just too much. After some tests, luckily, it was another bladder infection. When I got home, he was still asleep. The third time was in December — the birth was scheduled for 15 January (my father's birthday). This time the bleeding was a lot heavier and I was really scared. By chance, he was home — it freaked him out. Ultimately, it turned out to be yet another bladder infection. They, however, did keep me in the hospital for a few days. Surprisingly, he did not leave me. We were inside the house, almost constantly, awaiting the birth.

I knew that my baby was a boy. As I was already 39 when I fell pregnant, I had decided to undergo an amniocentesis. Did he come with me? No, it was my mum who was there when they placed the thick needle into my womb. When they called with the test results a few days later, I was thrilled to hear that the baby was okay. I had no preference as to a boy or a girl. I do recall thinking when they told me that it was a boy, "Wow, another person in the house that I will never fully understand." He was pleased though. A second son. Three kids. Bypassing that, he still had no or little contact with the other two.

The day before my due date, I went to the hospital for a

regular check-up. It had been snowing. I was stubborn, did not even think about taking a taxi. I had always walked fast. But now, any 95-year-old would have beaten me. When I got to the hospital, they noticed that my blood pressure was very high. I had never had high blood pressure before. They feared I had pre-eclampsia — or as we say in Dutch: pregnancy-poisoning — which is a dangerous condition. The game plan was for me to be admitted to hospital. They would test my urine for 24 hours and if I had pre-eclampsia, they would induce the birth. I called him. He came to the hospital with my little suitcase filled with clothes for me and the baby. As there was little or no sign of a birth yet, he ventured home. There I was. Alone. By chance, I spotted a colleague of mine visiting one of his friends in the room next door. I called out his name. Imagine being an active, 20-something, single bloke and somebody calling your name in the maternity ward! It was fun being able to speak to a 'real' person for a while. Yes, I had my mobile phone with me, but I was alone in that room. Alone... and afraid.

Night set in. At around 2am on which was now due date, January 15, I felt a cramp. I thought, "Okay, I must do a poo." Went to the toilet. Nothing. Okay. Five minutes later, another cramp. Back to the toilet. Nothing. Could it be a contraction? Surely not, they had not given me any medication to induce the birth yet. In the pregnancy course (I took the fast version, did not want to spend 12 weeks on it) they had talked about the pattern of contractions. A little cramp. Thirty to 40 minutes later, another one. And so on. Mine were heavy and every five minutes, right from the start. After timing these for an hour or so, I called a nurse. They noticed how regular the contractions already were and said, "Call your husband — this will not take long now." I called him around 5:30 am. He was still awake. Of course, he was. Night-time was his time. He took a taxi to the hospital. We waited. And waited.

The contractions were painful. Very painful. There was no time in between to regain my breath. Yet there was no dilation. I thought about the story my mum had told me about the birth of my oldest brother. A birth that lasted four long and painful days due to... no dilation. I was not going to last for four days. When we approached 2pm, I told the nurse, "I think it is time to think about pain relief." In the Netherlands, the approach is that birth should be as natural as possible.

"Would you like a brochure?" the nurse asked. A brochure? Was this an episode of Candid Camera? To date, this cracks up my medical friends.

"NO, I would like to see an anaesthesiologist."

As the anaesthesiologists were all caught up in the operating rooms, they first gave me a pethidine injection. My first try at drugs, EVER. I recall seeing the earth move as I had seen in LSD animations. I talked for hours in my sleep, saying stuff like, "I do not think I will go into the office today." By the way, my constant talking had annoyed him. He could not sleep because of me.

Finally, they gave me the epidural. It stopped the pain. It also slowed down the contractions. I was watching *The A-team* on TV. He was busy smoking outside the hospital and chatting to a salsa friend who was working in the hospital as a cleaner. The hours went by. And by. Until, at 10pm the doctor said, "The machine indicates that the baby's heartbeat is rising. As you do not have a fever, I do not know what the cause is. I want to go and 'collect him' if that is okay with you." I remember thinking, "You can drag him out of my ear if that would be easiest way to get him OUT." We went into the operating room. Notwithstanding the fact that his mum had been a doctor, he was scared stiff of hospitals, doctors, and blood. He said, "Sorry, but I cannot be there with you." Fine. He had not truly been there for me, ever. There I was. Alone. As they cut my belly open, him not being there slashed my heart in two. That wound will never heal again.

My son was born just before midnight on my father's birthday.

My son was okay. I was happy. He stayed for a while, until I had come out of the recovery room. Then he went home.

Normally, a father would just go home to have a shower and return instantly. He, however, got high. It was my mum who stopped by at the first visitor's hour at 11am, who gave my son his first bottle. He would not return until late in the afternoon. I spent four nights in the hospital. I was in a lot of pain, notwithstanding the morphine (my second and to date, final drugs experience). My mum came to visit as often as she could. So did friends and family members. He showed up for an hour or so each day. Too busy celebrating. We came home on a Tuesday morning. I was still unable to walk or even stand up straight. A few days later the caesarean wound cracked open. Friends who had been visiting us took me to ER. They stitched me up again — and later sent me a fine for not stopping at my GP first. I felt shit at being a mum, not being able to look after my son properly.

PAPA WAS A ROLLING STONE

If I can give him credit for anything, it is for having helped me during that first month after my son's birth. He did not go out; he did help me as much as he could. But once I was a bit more mobile again, he went back into his real life. The night life. Drugs. Drinks. Most probably women too. Not that I could find any evidence of him sleeping around — but in hindsight, I know that he had been seeing at least one ex. When my son was six months, he had finally arranged for his daughter and her mum to visit us. He had kept our relationship, even our wedding, a secret. But now he wanted the kids to meet. The daughter and my son, it was love at first sight. From a number of stories that he told us that day (if not to say, bragged about), his daughter's mother and I realised that he had been painting totally different time-line pictures to her, to me and to the mother of his other son. Whilst she and I were recovering from all this, his father called from Cuba. His mother, who had always been a bit of a drama queen, was supposedly dying, again. She loved to play the 'Let's not eat until I am fainting constantly' game. He would then fly over to visit her. A dangerous game but as a doctor, she knew exactly how far she could stretch it. He became hysterical and immediately packed his bags to catch the earliest flight. Leaving his new job (he lost jobs every other day) and leaving me behind with a six-month-old baby. Two weeks passed. I spoke to him occasionally. He seemed to be very busy. Visiting friends and stuff. His mum was a lot better now. They even shared his childhood bed together (to date, this freaks me out).

REHAB NO, NO, NO... YES

He seemed very happy when he got back. A bit weird though when it came to computers and the internet. He would venture out to internet cafes 'because our computer did not have a camera'. I was too exhausted to think about why he would need a camera. I was also too busy arranging for him to finally go to rehab. He had always loved Amy Winehouse's rehab song. I had made it clear, from the moment my son was born, that he had to clean up his act. It took a long time to organise. He had always resisted going. Strangely enough, he was all for it as soon as he came back from Cuba. In January, he finally left for Scotland a few days after my son's first birthday. I had suggested that I could come and visit him as soon as the programme would allow me to. No, that was not necessary. He had been very distant ever since coming back from Cuba. But I was too tied up in the working full time, looking after the baby and organising his shit that I had not really paid attention to it.

I did not have much hope that he would scrub up sufficiently to be a good husband and father — but at least, if it did not work out, I could later explain to my son that I had tried everything. Only a few friends knew that he had gone to rehab. Most folks around me never noticed — he had not been a part of my social life. It made no difference to my daily routine. If anything, I had more peace and quiet. And no drug debts to pay. His addiction bled me dry. Why did I keep paying? I did not want to put myself or my son in danger. Drug debts are dirty debts and the dealers knew where we lived.

I would call him in Scotland. Sometimes one of his roommates would answer (he was almost always out), "Hi, is this [unclear name]?" "No, this is [my name]." I thought nothing of it — there were many guys in that house, how would they remember each other's girlfriends' names? In the few brief calls, I asked how he was. Just fine. Truly.

June. It was his birthday. I was at work, working on a multi-billion transaction. I called him at the clinic. And then he told me, "Well, thank you for congratulating me. I want a divorce." Oops. It did not come as a total surprise. I had made it clear: either you can turn your shit around and become responsible or you are out. He beat me to it. But still, it hurt. A colleague stopped by in my room to discuss some paperwork. His girlfriend had only just left him, and he felt instantly that I was going through a similar thing. He got me a cup of tea, and together we worked hard at the transaction. As it got late, I asked my mum to get my son from the nursery and take a taxi to my office. I had told her that he had mentioned divorce and that I might need her to come back home with me for support. My son was running around happily in the office, I closed the deal, we took a taxi home and I said to my mum, "It is cool. You can go to your house. I have got this." My son went to sleep, and I sat down at the computer to write the first draft of a divorce agreement. Perks of being a lawyer and having been through a divorce once before. There were no more tears left.

GOING TO MIAMI

When he got back from rehab in July, he did stay at our house whilst we were waiting for a lawyer friend of mine to finalise the paperwork for the divorce. That guy was going to come to our house on a Saturday afternoon. The night before, out of the blue, he said, "I am moving to Miami."

"What?"

"Yeah, I need to be away from Amsterdam — too many drugs."

"Are you kidding me?" I said. "In the 80s when you were listening to Fidel Castro every single night, we were watching *Miami Vice*. A world unknown to us. Some teens smoked pot. But cocaine was not a regular thing in Amsterdam back then. If you do not want to be exposed to drugs, Miami is the worst destination imaginable. And, have you forgotten that you have three children in the Netherlands?"

He still wanted to go.

"Well, if you want to go, go."

We signed the paperwork and he awaited his visa. I wondered who paid for his ticket. I certainly had not.

August. 7am. He came home from a night on the town as I was getting ready to take my son to the nursery and go to work. I heard him downstairs. Screaming. Throwing things. In all the time I knew him (okay, we met, married, became parents, and divorced within 3.5 years), he had never been aggressive. Until that morning. He scared me. Here my experience with the abuser came in handy. I calculated: so many steps down the stairs, to my bag, to the door... He accused me of all sorts. I had always been a bad fuck. I had abused him. As had so many other women. And like the mothers of the other kids, I had basically bought my kid from him. Something snapped deep inside of me but I kept my cool. I made sure that my son and I got out of the door safely. As we stood in the public hallway, I whispered at him, soft but clearly, "I will get back at 5:30pm. Either you are gone, or you will die." Many men have said many things to me, but nobody can just tell me that I bought my child. I love that little boy with everything that I have. He is, and will always be, my biggest treasure. A gift from the universe.

I got home at 5:30pm. He had left. Taken his clothes. His phone was switched off. In the weeks that followed, I could tell he was not using his bank card nor his public transport card. I figured he had left for Miami. By then, I was not using Facebook. But he had been. So very cleverly, I typed 'Facebook' into the browser of our computer. He had not logged out... and I found a chat between him and a friend of his in Cuba. He had landed in Miami alright! Man, how many ladies wanted kinky sex there, it was a paradise. "Hey mate, you remember that goddess that I met again when I was in Cuba last year? The girl from the hood? That sensual angel? Well I am with her now. Life is beautiful." I felt like throwing up. I should have guessed. It did not give me any pleasure reading that within days of arriving there, he had already cheated on his Cuban angel. I do not hold her accountable, at all, for him leaving us and moving there. No doubt he had told her stories like, "Our marriage is basically over, but we are staying together for the kid." Stories that she wanted to believe. As I had once believed his stories too.

I told his once and my now best friend about the move. He said, "Miami? Do you know who moved there recently? Martha." He had told me about Martha. She had been the sort of love of his life. But he claimed that his best friend had told awful lies about him to Martha. And they split up. Obviously, from the friend, I know that they split up for totally different reasons. As I found out later, while we were together, he was still seeing her. She often would visit the restaurant where he was then working, at the corner of our house. Same old, same old. Fancy that — he and Martha both living in Miami. A coincidence?

HEY, HOW ARE YOU DOING?

Months passed. He finally phoned me in December. He was well surprised when I told him that I knew about her. About him and her. He had been asking, "So how is this and that person and he and she and whomever?" Then I said, "Tell me, how is she [name of that girl]?" He fell silent. I hung up the phone. I tried to keep the communication going via messenger. But it was, as ever, all about him. I tried to tell him about my son's life, about the difficulties I was facing. I was a single, full time working mum. He never cared. Never paid any alimony.

At thanksgiving, he suggested a Skype call, early morning Amsterdam time. My son was almost three. He had no clue who this fellow was and chose to watch kids' TV instead. He had about ten other Cubans there, who were dancing wildly. When he asked me how my mum was, I told him in Cuban slang that she, notwithstanding her age, would love to slash his throat for what he had done to me and my son. The Cubans stopped their dancing, looking at me with a mixture of fear and admiration. That is the last time I spoke to him. Ever.

SERIAL FATHER

Meanwhile, the mother of the half-brother got in

touch. She felt comfortable for her son to meet his siblings. The mother of the half-daughter also loved the idea of the kids meeting each other. We all met at my apartment. The children instantly bonded and they have a great bond to date. What I had hoped in the beginning, that by having a child with him, I would not lose his children in a breakup, I have achieved. We are a very modern family.

He has a fourth child now with this Cuban angel. He had mentioned, before setting off to Miami, that he might consider having another child. Whilst when I had my son, he kept saying, "No more. Never again." I had told him truthfully, "That would be a bad idea. Is it your fantasy to one day take all your kids to Disneyland, provided they can all fit into one minivan? You could have a picture of you printed on their t-shirts." He thought that was very unkind of me to say. So, he had his fourth child. A boy. Perhaps he has finally learned that having a child comes with a huge responsibility. I am not keeping my hopes up. Earlier this year, he mentioned to a joint friend that he wanted to leave Miami and return to the Netherlands to be with his family. To which our friend replied, "Which of the three families are you referring to?".

A serial father, that is what he is. Now that would make for a great book. The other two mothers and I are still debating who should play him in the movie adaptation. I do have the final scene in mind. Imagine a regular Florida condo with a big pond. There is this guy, sneaking away from a garden in the middle of a night, blowing a kiss to a woman on the porch. "Ciao, guapa." He walks around the pond. He stops. What is this soft growling sound? Suddenly, an alligator appears from the deep dark waters. A scream. And then, the sound of silence…

Life After Him

My story may have sounded familiar to you. Awfully familiar. You too were once a very independent lady. That is how you knew yourself. How your friends, family and co-workers knew you. Very independent, very strong, very successful, very out there, very much enjoying life.

Then he came along. The one that swept you from your feet. The one in control. His confidence attracted you. He knew so many things, so many people. Wow. What a guy. He lured you into a dance. Into a relationship. You loved for him to lead you – to new places, to new highs. Whenever you offered to do something, to arrange for something, he waved it away. He was the man. He would take care of you. You let your guard down. Bit by bit. He knew how to creep under your skin. Like a spider. Bite by bite.

At the office, you were still you. Making important

decisions. With confidence. Yet at home, well that is a different story. He called the shots. He made you feel like you knew nothing. He used every single moment to make you feel small. He called you names. Made you question your reality. Once the fire started to cool down, you started to feel suffocated. You had become so dependent on him, as if you had no will of your own.

When you had reached your lightbulb NO MORE moment, when you managed to escape, all you wished for was to be independent again. One hundred per cent. Not allowing anybody near you, not listening to any suggestions. No-one was to be trusted after all.

You would deal with the memories, as you had always dealt with everything – work, friendship, family. Fully independent. Yet it turned out to be hard. Hard to be alone with these memories. Who could you share them with? This had not happened to anybody you knew. Especially not to other successful, professional women. Surely not to any of your colleagues. Who to turn to? How to build up YOUR life again?

I have been there.

After the divorce from the addict, I did not immediately deal with the hurt. As a single mum, working 40 hours per week, I had little time to process what had happened. I carried on. No time to think. No time to feel. Then, as my son got a bit older and I had a bit more time, the memories started to creep in on me. I hardly slept a wink, going from nightmare to nightmare. I knew the time had come to deal with the pain, the anger, the hate.

What did I do? I sought help. Professional help AND support from friends. Who, as it turned out, had many similar tales to tell.

Men-wise, did I find love after the HIMs? I met up again with my first ever love. A love before any of the HIMs in the book. We had a small pause of 26-years, in which we both matured. Now we live together with my son and his oldest daughter. This blend is as shaken and stirred as a martini – but equally just as tasty and sizzling!

DISCLAIMER

Each story is different. Each healing journey will also be different. There is not a quick **How to Survive a Toxic Relationship** fix. I am not a counsellor, nor a therapist. I speak from my experience with the sole aim to raise awareness on abuse and to make you and other women realise that you are not the only person that this has happened to. I cannot wave a magic wand and say: if you do this, this, and this, then you will be healed. There are several routes to heal – and you must find the one right for

DO NOT TRY HIM AT HOME

you. Counselling and peer support helped me tremendously.

COUNSELLING

The counsellor helped me to gain insight into questions such as:

- Why was I drawn to the dynamics of an abusive relationship?
- Why did I ignore the red flags?
- Why did I allow these men to overstep my boundaries – time and time again?

The answers were to be found in family dynamics. I come from a long line of unholy unions between alcoholics and co-dependents. Unions that all ended in divorce. When my parents split up, I developed a huge fear of rejection. I was an easy target at primary school. The other kids bullied me to the point that I contemplated running away from home – or worse. When I entered the wondrous world of romantic relationships, my self-esteem was very low. My fear of abandonment, however, was very high. I was so happy that a guy, any guy, would pay attention to me that I did not react instantly when red flags appeared. The HIMs scared me. But I was still more scared of ending up alone.

There were so many signs and red flags, that I chose to ignore. There was abuse on so many levels: emotionally, physically, and financially.

What the HIMs all had in common:

- They had no money, no house, no education, no security. Which meant that they moved in with me just after meeting me and made me pay for everything. All their bills and all their desires.
- They lied – about everything and anything, up to the colour of the socks they were wearing.
- They slept around with other women, structurally.
- They made me question my mind, my memory and my behaviour.
- The abuser and the addict were both addicted to cocaine and sex.

The abuser added many more layers of abuse.

- He called me names and talked badly about me to others.
- He hit me and tried to kill me.
- He made me beg for forgiveness, while I had done nothing wrong.
- He forbade me to say or do a lot of things.
- He isolated me from my friends and family.

- He forced me to perform sexual acts that I was not comfortable with.
- He abandoned me in public places.
- He demanded access to my mobile phone and laptop.

The counsellor helped me to see the patterns and to slowly build up my self-esteem. I had lost trust in myself and the world. My confidence had been shattered. By focusing on what I had achieved, what I was doing right, who I could trust, my mindset shifted. Yes, I may have been drawn to a certain kind of guy BUT the abuse was not my fault. It never had been. They were 100 per cent responsible for their behaviour and their actions. I learned to forgive myself. To be kind to myself. To give myself the love that I had sought outside myself for too long. How? By changing my narrative. Whenever I felt myself slipping into 'it was all my fault' or 'I am worthless', I would pause and say, "Is that really true? Is this me talking or my inner critic?" This innate old, muppet voice still comes up – but I now recognise it much earlier and know how to silence it.

PEER SUPPORT

Counselling brought me back to my core values. Made me appreciate myself. I still felt a tad alone though. Surely there were not many other professional women who had endured an abusive relationship. That void, that sense of being all alone, could not be filled by counselling alone.

As my confidence grew, I started to talk about my story. Bit by bit. Friend by friend. Then more and more friends started to tell me, "It happened to me too." All professional, high achieving women. Like me, they had thought they were the only ones that this had ever happened to. Like me, they were convinced that it had been their fault.

Just by comparing our stories, by showing mutual compassion, our paradigms shifted. We were able to view our stories through a different lens. We all suffered from a low self-esteem caused by unsafe situations in our childhood. But on top of that, we discovered a communal pattern of feeling less than human. Of feeling less deserving.

CONDITIONING

We dug deep and discovered layers of conditioning: to upkeep the image of the good girl, we allowed shit from men. Good to whom? Certainly not to us. By pleasing these guys, by pleasing society, we lost ourselves. Nobody taught us to set safe and sound boundaries. To walk away, straight away, if a man would disrespect us. We did not learn how to trust our gut, always. If only we had known how to see behind the shiny 'Too Good to Be True' façade. How to, without hesitation, leave a man who makes us feel uncomfortable. Undesirable. Unwanted. Undeserving.

For too long we had believed in fairy tales. The damsel in distress, in need of salvation. Marrying the first prince who kissed us. Taking shit because we were told to stand by our man. We were brainwashed. Where we grew professionally, we stayed little girls when it came to romance. A disaster waiting to happen....

We cannot undo our upbringing. Nor unread or unhear all the messages that have made us stay with toxic men for too long. But we can decide to, from now on, stand by ourselves. To please ourselves. To recognise our worth, to guard our boundaries and to accept nothing but a partner that is truly good for us. Love does not hurt. Control hurts. Abuse hurts. I set myself free, my friends set themselves free. I wish the same for all of you.

COMMUNITY

I decided to write this book to raise awareness of professional women being abused. Would there be something else that I could do to add support and to aid the healing journey? Yes, there is. I created a Facebook community group called Dare to Displease.

https://www.facebook.com/groups/daretodisplease/

Dare to Displease is a secure haven, which is growing into a supportive community of women who have survived toxic relationships. Who are taking positive steps, every single day, to build better lives for themselves. The keywords of the group are: SUPPORT, PRIVACY, and INTERDEPENDENCE. Creating a safe bond. We can rely on each other, but we will maintain our identities. Working together on our own paths!

Owning our stories. Taking responsibility. This is in no way a victimhood worshipping or ex-bashing place. It is all about us. About our strength and our future.

With me as a facilitating lighthouse who provides the tools, tips, and tricks. You will do the sailing at your own pace. Daring to venture just a bit further away from the shore every single week. Knowing that the lighthouse is always there to bring you home again. Home to you. I would be honoured if you would join us there. A warm welcome awaits you.

Resources

If you are or have been in an abusive relationship or suspect that a friend or loved one is being abused, there is a great number of organisations that can help you. Never feel ashamed to reach out for help!

WHAT IS ABUSE?

Extensive list of examples of abuse (physical, emotional, sexual, financial, digital):

- http://safehavenshelter.org/learn/educational-resources/domestic-violence/examples-of-abuse/

Clear insight into the cycle of abuse:

- https://www.helpguide.org/articles/abuse/domestic-violence-and-abuse.htm

HELPLINES

WHEN IN IMMEDIATE DANGER, RING THE NATIONAL EMERGENCY NUMBER:

- USA – 911
- UK — 999
- EU — 112
- Australia – 000 or 112 (when calling with a mobile phone)
- New Zealand — 111

FOR ASSISTANCE REGARDING (THE AFTERMATH OF) ABUSE:

USA

- http://safehavenshelter.org/services/
- https://www.thehotline.org/

UK

- https://www.womensaid.org.uk/information-support/
- https://www.gov.uk/report-domestic-abuse

Netherlands

- https://www.huiselijkgeweld.nl/

- https://www.ikvermoedhuiselijkgeweld.nl/

Australia

- https://protectivegroup.com.au/about/
- https://www.whiteribbon.org.au/find-help/domestic-violence-hotlines/

New Zealand

- https://www.govt.nz/browse/law-crime-and-justice/abuse-harassment-domestic-violence/domestic-and-family-violence/
- http://www.areyouok.org.nz/family-violence/statistics/

REACH OUT TO ME

If you are in doubt where to go or what to do, reach me:

Facebook group:
https://www.facebook.com/groups/daretodisplease/

Facebook book page:
https://www.facebook.com/DoNotTryHIMatHome/

LinkedIn:
https://www.linkedin.com/in/sandratenhoope/

DO NOT TRY HIM AT HOME

DO NOT TRY HIM AT HOME

Lightning Source UK Ltd.
Milton Keynes UK
UKHW021210210920
370268UK00017B/1773

9 781838 163402